Who Is Jesus?

~

A Journal Bible Study
For Beginners and Seekers

Includes the Complete Gospel of Mark

SANDY K. COOK

Published by Psalm 30 Publishing,
© 2018 Sandra K. Cook, All rights reserved.

Cover Photo credit: https://www.pexels.com/@zozz, "Sunflower Garden Under Blue Sky," used under Free to use, public domain open license, with no attribution required.

ISBN: 978-1-948953-04-7

Psalm 30 Publishing,
P.O. Box 491328,
Lawrenceville, GA 30049

Unless otherwise noted, Bible verses printed in this book are taken from translations of the Bible that are freely available in the Public Domain. Verses have been taken from an ASV-based, Public Domain translation, and have been modified to eliminate the use of the formal name of God. Within this book, God is addressed as God, The Lord, or Jesus throughout the book. As required by the Public Domain permissions of the secondary Public Domain source, the specific secondary Public Domain source will remain unidentified in this publication, because some of the verses have been modified and the verses no longer directly reflect the content of that specific public domain source.

DEDICATION

This book is dedicated to Seekers of God. It is dedicated to YOU, because you are searching for God and His truth. I pray God will open your eyes fully and give you great insights into His truths and His ways through this study. ♥

This book is also dedicated to my Christian brothers and sisters. You have helped me travel an amazing road of spiritual growth. You, my friends, inspire me and keep me moving toward heaven's righteousness to come. ♥

And lastly, with the utmost of thankfulness, it is dedicated to Jesus, who is the world's Lord and Savior. ♥

ACKNOWLEDGMENTS

First and foremost, I'd like to acknowledge Jesus Christ, as my Lord and Savior, who led me along this path to becoming a writer, God who gave me spiritual gifts of knowledge, faith, and teaching, and the Holy Spirit, who helped me stay focused, gave me insights, and helped me keep moving forward. Without the Divine Trinity in my life, I'd still be wondering what is the purpose of my life, and surely would not have designed this Bible study. 🕊

Second, I would like to acknowledge those who have helped me edit and craft this Journal Bible Study as an introduction to Jesus. In particular, I'd like to thank the members of my Global Girls' 90 Day Challenge mentoring group. You have each encouraged me and kept me on track during the ups and downs of daily life. Without you, this book may never have been completed. So, I thank you with all of my heart. ♥

Table of Contents

A LOOK BEFORE YOU LEAP

Who is Jesus that people care about Him more than 2000 years after He lived? Jesus wasn't wealthy. The Bible says He wasn't good looking. He wasn't royalty, a government official, or even a church leader during His time on Earth. In fact, church leaders hated Jesus back then, and lots of people still hate Jesus. WHY?

What is it about Jesus that makes people either LOVE Him or hate Him? What about you? Would you love Jesus or hate Him if you met Him today?

This is one question you will be better able to answer after reading this book and journaling your thoughts. At the end of this study, you'll have a much clearer idea about who Jesus is, and you're highly likely to have stronger feelings about Him, one way or another.

It's important to note: If Jesus lied about Himself and God, then Jesus can't possibly be a "great prophet," as some people believe. Truly great prophets don't lie. If Jesus told the truth in all He said, then we really need to listen to and learn from Him. So here's another decision you'll be able to make: Is Jesus telling the truth? If so, what weight do His words carry for you today?

Come and travel with Jesus, as the story of His life unfolds in the Book of Mark. Spend time here, with Jesus, and get to know Him. See what you think. Will you stand with the crowd, yelling, "Crucify Him! Crucify Him!" or will you be like a robber on a cross, asking Jesus if you can spend your eternity with Him? On this journey you will learn Who Is Jesus, and you'll decide if He matters to you.

What Kind of Bible Study is This?

This is an open-ended, reflective, and life application Journal Bible Study. It's a combination book, journal, and workbook. The study is open-ended and reflective because it is designed to let God's Holy Spirit teach you what He wants YOU to know.

In this study you won't find lengthy explanations about each passage. You won't find my interpretations or strong direction about how you should think of the Bible verses themselves. Instead, you are encouraged to pray and ask God to give you insight into His word.

If you use this study in a Bible study group, then discussing what each person discovered can be enlightening, because everyone gets something different out of a study like this. If you don't have a group to gather with, that's okay. You can use any resource you want to do some research and better your understanding. However, you'll also find you can gain insight and understanding by rereading the texts for meaning. God made the Bible to be understood by common people, like you and me.

What you get out of each chapter will be between you and God. Your takeaways will depend on your life and circumstances, as well as how purposefully you seek to understand God's Word as you read.

This is also a God-directed Bible study. In other words, as you read, pray and ask God for insight. Ask Him to show you the things He wants you to see. God will bring to your mind ideas and truths which are personally meaningful to you.

One of the main features of this Bible study is the inclusion of the actual Bible text. All you need is this book and a pen or pencil, because the full Gospel of Mark is included.

The inclusion of the Bible text itself serves two purposes. It makes the study more convenient, because you don't have to go back-and-forth between this book and a Bible. You can read the text and answer questions right where you are in this journal. As long as you have this journal and something to write with, you have all you need.

The second purpose for including the text is for simplicity in studying, especially for anyone who is new to Bible studies. It's difficult and time-consuming to find passages in a Bible, especially if you're unfamiliar with the Bible's layout. Having to look up a lot of scriptures can affect a readers' ability to follow the story being told.

By including the Bible text in this Journal, you can read without stopping. You won't have to go back-and-forth between the journal and a Bible. Therefore, you should find this Journal Bible Study quite easy to use.

That said, it's great for anyone who really wants to know God's Word to get an actual Bible to read. All of the Bible, taken as a whole, is critical for understanding God's grand story. No scripture should be considered a complete work in isolation from the rest of the

Bible, including this study.

Because we need to know God's whole story, this Journal Bible Study is just one book in a series. While each of these journals isn't a complete work by itself apart from the Holy Bible, the individual journals in this series make studying the Bible easier.

If you don't have a Bible to read, you can find virtual Bibles at BibleGateway.com or Bible.com. If you'd like help selecting a Bible version that's easy for you to read, visit: christianonlinebiblestudy.com/how-to-choose-a-bible/

Information on that webpage will teach you how to select a version which will be easy for you to use. It has samples of a variety of translations. Hopefully, you'll be able to find a translation that appeals to you.

How To Use This Journal Bible Study

In this Journal Bible Study, each chapter is one chapter in the Gospel Book of Mark in the New Testament. Since Mark's manuscript was originally written without verse numbers, the verse numbers have been removed from the text shared in this book.

Removing verse numbers lets your reading flow, as if you are reading a story. The Gospels tell the story of Jesus' life, so reading Mark as a story is more natural.

Next to each column of text, there is a wide margin for notetaking or journaling. This margin is designed for you to write down *anything* that comes to mind as you read. You can use the journal area to:

- Make notes about questions you have,
- Express your emotions and reactions to the events of the story,
- Record your thoughts about Jesus' teachings and actions,
- Make note of commands Jesus gives about what to do and what not to do,
- Express how you feel the text relates to your life or personality,
- Or any thought you have that comes to mind while you're reading.

If you like to draw or use color, the open space allows you the freedom to draw, do lettering or interact with the Bible texts in any way you find helpful.

The best way to use this type of study is to settle in where you'll be comfortable and can hopefully read a chapter without interruption. Before you begin reading, take a few minutes to pray.

Praying is simply talking to God, as if He were a friend sitting next to you. Since God is Spirit, He is with us at all times wherever we go, and He will hear whatever you say or ask. You may want to pray something similar to this:

"Dear Lord, please open my mind and speak to my heart where I need to be touched. Help me see Jesus for who He truly is, and reveal Yourself to me. Give me the knowledge and understanding I need through this study. I ask these things in the name of Jesus, Amen."

After praying, you might find it helpful to start by reading the "**WHAT'S NEXT?**" section at the end of the previous chapter, especially if it's been a few days since you last read. Taking a few moments for review can help you reconnect with the main focus for the chapter you are about to read.

Read the day's chapter, while making notes and expressing yourself in the space provided. Freely write whatever comes to your mind.

At the end of each chapter, you will find a "**DID YOU NOTICE?**" section with thoughts for you to ponder. Consider the focus points of the chapter for a moment, then write down your personal reaction or thoughts in the space provided.

The focus points are followed by a series of reflective study questions in the "**WHAT DO YOU THINK?**" section. This is an opportunity to consider how the chapter's content applies to your life, actions, thoughts, and feelings. Make this study personal. Make it about you and your relationship with God.

Take the scriptures into your heart and really think about what the Bible verses mean to you personally. Consider what God may want YOU to know. Then thoughtfully answer each of the reflection questions.

If you have no immediate reaction or thought, pray over the question. Ask God for His insight. Ask Him to bring to your mind ideas about how the information applies to you.

Quiet your mind and spirit for a moment, and wait for meaningful insight to come into your mind or heart. Then take note of thoughts the Holy Spirit brings to you. I find that pausing and reflecting on the question often brings things to mind which are particularly meaningful to me.

There is an "**ACTION ITEM**" after the questions, which is designed to help you implement actions based on what you've learned. I will be up front, and tell you, these action items often assume you believe in God. If you don't, that's FINE! Just skip the action items. You can also skip any question you don't feel is applicable to you in your life circumstances, or due to your beliefs. The Action Items and questions are here to help you get more out of the study, but are not meant to be legalistic. There is no expectation that you must answer the questions.

Lastly, each chapter has a "**WHAT'S NEXT?**" section. This is a preview of the upcoming chapter. In this section, you'll find brief insights into the next chapter's main event(s), main point(s) or points worth noting. This section is designed to help you transition your mind from one chapter to the next.

On that note, let's look at "**WHAT'S NEXT?**" for the first chapter of this Journal Bible Study:

In the first chapter you will meet Jesus. When the Book of Mark begins, Jesus is already an adult. He is beginning to teach in the synagogues, begins speaking publicly, and He starts reaching out to individual people.

Jesus appears on the scene and starts telling people, "Follow Me," and amazingly, they DO exactly that!

Something to consider: If Jesus walked up to you and said, "Follow Me," would you drop everything and follow Him? There were at least 12 men who did that.

It's important to note: all of those who followed Jesus were men of the Jewish faith who knew the Messiah was coming. They believed Jesus was the person for which they were waiting, so they immediately followed Jesus.

Before we dive into the Good News of Jesus, let's talk a little bit about Mark (a.k.a. John Mark), who is the author of the Book of Mark.

Who is Mark?

Mark was a traveling companion of the Apostles Paul and Peter. Mark introduces us to Jesus in his Gospel account of Jesus' life through his book.

Mark, or John Mark as he's also known, is mentioned in five chapters of the New Testament in the Bible. Here's what we know about Mark directly from the Bible:

Acts 12:12 – *"Thinking about that, he (Peter) came to the house of Mary, the mother of John who was called **Mark**, where many were gathered together and were praying."*

In this first reference to Mark, we see that people gathered in Mark's mother's home. His mother, Mary, hosted gatherings for people to pray together. From this passage, we know Mark came from a home where religion was important, and where believers gathered together to pray.

Acts 12:25 – *"Barnabas and Saul returned to Jerusalem, when they had fulfilled their service, also taking with them John who was called **Mark**."*

Barnabas and Saul went on a missionary journey to tell people the Good News about Jesus. Mark was a traveling companion of theirs. Saul's name was later changed to Paul, and he wrote more of the books in the New Testament than any other author. There is no doubt Mark learned a lot about Jesus during his travels with Barnabas and Saul.

Acts 15:36-40 - *"After some days Paul said to Barnabas, 'Let's return now and visit our brothers in every city in which we proclaimed the word of the Lord, to see how they* *are doing.' Barnabas planned to take John, who was called **Mark**, with them also. But Paul didn't think that it was a good idea to take with them someone who had withdrawn from them in Pamphylia, and didn't go with them to do the work.*

*"Then the contention grew so sharp that they separated from each other. Barnabas took **Mark** with him, and sailed away to Cyprus, but Paul chose Silas, and went out, being commended by the brothers to the grace of God."*

Here, we see that Paul wasn't always happy with John Mark. We don't know exactly what happened, but we know that Mark withdrew from Paul and Barnabas, while they were in Pamphylia. Apparently that really upset Paul, so he no longer wanted to travel with Mark.

Thus, Mark became the main traveling companion of Barnabas for a while. The issues between Mark and Paul disappeared over time. Mark and Paul's relationship became close again, as you will see in the next few verses.

Colossians 4:10-11 – In these verses, Paul is writing to the Colossian people. Paul wrote, *"Aristarchus, my fellow prisoner, greets you, and **Mark**, the cousin of Barnabas (concerning whom you received commandments, "if he comes to you, receive him"), and Jesus who is called Justus. These are my only fellow workers for God's Kingdom who are of the circumcision, men who have been a comfort to me."*

In this passage, it is clear Mark is with Paul while Paul is in prison. Paul refers to Mark as one of his "fellow workers for God's Kingdom." Paul also says the men mentioned, including Mark, are a comfort to him. From this scripture we know Paul has a better relationship with Mark than he did previously.

In this verse, we also learn Mark is a cousin of Barnabas. Therefore, it makes sense that Barnabas traveled with Mark when Barnabas and Paul split and went on different missionary journeys.

Paul refers to his fellow workers, including Mark, as being "of the circumcision." From that statement, knowing God commanded Jews to be circumcised in the Old Testament, we can deduce Mark is a Jewish man.

2 Timothy 4:11 – 2 Timothy is a letter Paul wrote to Timothy when Paul was in prison. Paul was a spiritual father to Timothy, and Timothy was like a son to Paul. Paul writes to Timothy, *"Only Luke is with me. Get **Mark**, and bring him with you, for he is useful to me for service."*

In this part of the letter, Paul is giving instructions to Timothy. He is asking Timothy to bring certain items to him in prison, including parchment, his cloak, and Mark! Clearly Mark was useful to Paul at this point in his life, possibly because Mark served as Paul's scribe. We know from this passage, Mark and Paul had a good working relationship, which Paul valued in his later years.

Lastly, in 1 Peter, we see Mark is an important person in the Apostle Peter's life too:

1 Peter 5:12-14 - *"Through Silvanus, our faithful brother, as I consider him, I have written to you briefly, exhorting, and testifying that this is the true grace of God in which you stand. She who is in Babylon, chosen together with you, greets you; and **so does Mark, my son**. Greet one another with a kiss of love. Peace be to you all who are in Christ Jesus. Amen."*

This letter, written by Peter, he calls Mark his son. As a spiritual son to Peter, Mark undoubtedly earned the respect of Apostle Peter.

Mark learned a lot about Jesus—maybe more from Peter than from any other person. Why?

Peter was a fisherman, and he was an Apostle chosen directly by Jesus. Peter knew Jesus throughout His ministry on Earth, and experienced life with Jesus first-hand. As an eye-witness to every aspect of Jesus' ministry on earth, Peter was more qualified to speak about what Jesus said and did than anyone else, as were the other eleven original apostles.

Mark would have learned a lot from Peter because of Peter's close, direct friendship with Jesus. As someone who worked closely with both Apostles, Paul and Peter, Mark can be considered an authoritative speaker about Jesus' teachings and His life.

As Apostle Paul's traveling companion, Mark learned virtually everything Paul taught. As Apostle Peter's spiritual son, Mark undoubtedly heard many of Peter's first-hand accounts about all Jesus said and did.

Therefore, Mark is one of the most qualified early Christians to write a book about Jesus' teachings, miracles, and the events surrounding Jesus' life. Mark is able to give a detailed account of what Jesus did and said during His adult life on earth.

Mark's Authority

As a side note, we don't know for certain if Mark knew Jesus personally. It's certainly possible, since Mark's life is likely to have overlapped Jesus' ministry on earth. If Mark actually met Jesus, Mark would have been a young man at the time.

Each of the four Gospel books in the New Testament are well-documented as early, authentic documents. Mark's Gospel was written around 35 years after Jesus was crucified, and it was written within the lifetimes of many eye-witnesses who actually knew Jesus. Therefore, Mark's book is considered a highly reliable document about Jesus.

All four Gospels were written during the lifetimes of people who actually knew Jesus. You can see the New Testament books' dating at:

The four Gospel books are titled Matthew, Mark, Luke, and John, and they are found in the New Testament section of the Bible.

First century writings of a secular nature also reference the Gospel of Mark. This helps assure us Mark's book is an authentic writing from the first century.

My hope in developing this Journal Bible Study is that you will receive the Good News in Mark's Gospel with great joy. Whether or not the Good News impacts your life in a significant way will depend on you, your desire for a connection with God, how much you believe what Jesus said, and whether you pray for insight and understanding.

I hope you become inspired by the Good News in the Gospel message and find this is a worthwhile journey through the Book of Mark.

Are you ready to meet Jesus? Let's go..

1 NEWS OF JESUS SPREADS

The beginning of the Good News of Jesus Christ, the Son of God. As it is written in the prophets, "Behold, I send my messenger before your face, who will prepare your way before you: the voice of one crying in the wilderness, 'Make ready the way of the Lord! Make his paths straight!' "

John came baptizing in the wilderness and preaching the baptism of repentance for forgiveness of sins. All the country of Judea and all those of Jerusalem went out to him. They were baptized by him in the Jordan river, confessing their sins. John was clothed with camel's hair and a leather belt around his waist. He ate locusts and wild honey. He preached, saying, "After me comes he who is mightier than I, the thong of whose sandals I am not worth to stoop down and loosen.

I baptized you in water, but he will baptize you in the Holy Spirit."

In those days, Jesus came from Nazareth of Galilee, and was baptized by John in the Jordan river. Immediately coming up from the water, he saw the heavens parting, and the Spirit descending on him like a dove. A voice came out of the sky, *"You are my beloved Son, in whom I am well pleased."*

Immediately the Spirit drove him (Jesus) out into the wilderness. He was there in the wilderness forty days tempted by Satan. He was with the wild animals; and the angels were serving him.

Now after John was taken into custody, Jesus came into Galilee, preaching the Good News of God's Kingdom, and saying, *"The time is fulfilled, and God's Kingdom is at hand! Repent, and believe in the Good News."*

Passing along by the sea of Galilee, Jesus saw Simon and Andrew, the brother of Simon, casting a net into the sea, for they were fishermen. Jesus said to them, *"Come after me, and I will make you into fishers for men."*

Immediately they left their nets, and followed him. Going on a little further from there, he saw James the son of Zebedee, and John, his brother, who were also in the boat, called them, and they left their father, Zebedee, in the boat with the hired servants, and went after him.

They went into Capernaum, and immediately on the Sabbath day Jesus entered into the synagogue and taught.

They were astonished at his teaching, for he taught them as having authority, and not as the scribes. Immediately there was in their synagogue a man with an unclean spirit, and he cried out, saying, "Ha! What do we have to do with you, Jesus, you Nazarene? Have you come to destroy us? I know you who you are: the Holy One of God!"

Jesus rebuked him, saying, *"Be quiet, and come out of him!"*

The unclean spirit, convulsing him and crying with a loud voice, came out of him. They were all amazed, so that they questioned among themselves, saying, "What is this? A new teaching? For with authority he commands even the unclean spirits, and they obey him!" The report of Jesus went out immediately everywhere into all the region of Galilee and its surrounding area.

Immediately, when they had come out of the synagogue, they came into the house of Simon and Andrew, with James and John. Now Simon's wife's mother lay sick with a fever, and immediately they told Jesus about her. He came and took her by the hand, and raised her up. The fever left her immediately, and she served them.

At evening, when the sun had set, they brought to him all who were sick, and those who were possessed by demons. All the city was gathered together at the door. He healed many who were sick with various diseases, and cast out many demons. He didn't allow the demons to speak, because they knew him.

Early in the morning, while it was still dark, Jesus rose up and went out, and departed into a deserted place, and prayed there. Simon and those who were with him searched for him. They found him and told him, "Everyone is looking for you."

Jesus said to them, *"Let's go elsewhere into the next towns, that I may preach there also, because I came out for this reason."* He went into their synagogues throughout all Galilee, preaching and casting out demons. A leper came to him, begging him, kneeling down to him, and saying to him, "If you want to, you can make me clean."

Being moved with compassion, Jesus stretched out his hand, and touched the leper, and said to him, *"I want to. Be made clean."*

When Jesus had said this, immediately the leprosy departed from the leper, and he was made clean. Jesus strictly warned him, and immediately sent him out, and said to him, *"See you say nothing to anybody, but go show yourself to the priest, and offer for your cleansing the things which Moses commanded, for a testimony to them."*

But the man went out, and began to proclaim it much, and to spread about the matter, so that Jesus could no more openly enter into a city, but was outside in desert places. People came to him from everywhere.

DID YOU NOTICE?

In this opening chapter, we have a glimpse of what Jesus was doing when people began to notice Him. We read about John the Baptist's declaration that Jesus will baptize people with the Holy Spirit. What does that mean? It means we receive the indwelling spirit of God when we commit to following Jesus.

This opening chapter from the Book of Mark doesn't tell us about Jesus' birth and childhood, but other books of the Bible tell us about His beginning of life.

Jesus was born into a carpenter's family. As far as society goes, Jesus' family was a typical Jewish family. They weren't wealthy. They weren't famous. They weren't powerful. They were members of a small community with nothing notable about them, other than they were descendants of King David from long ago.

Since He was from a humble family background, as Jesus began to heal people and teach in synagogues, people were wondering, "Who is this JESUS guy?" People didn't know what to think about John and Jesus, but they were attracted to the teachings of these two men.

In those days, there was no broadcast media, mass produced newspapers, phones, or any other means for spreading news quickly. News spread solely by word of mouth. The news of Jesus began to spread with excitement. People might say:

"Jesus cured a lady's illness instantly, and He made a leper's leprosy disappear simply by taking him by the hand."

"Jesus drove out a demon by commanding it to leave!"

"Have you heard Jesus teaching? His teaching is astonishing, yet He's never had any formal education."

As a simple carpenter's son, Jesus quickly become a celebrity in the area. People sought Jesus out, because they wanted to see Him for themselves. Some sought Jesus to experience His miracles.

What would you do if you heard about Jesus and His miracles coming to your town? Would you seek to hear Jesus speak? What would you tell others about Him?

_____

_____

_____

_____

_____

_____

_____

WHAT DO YOU THINK?

➤ If you were alive when Jesus began healing and teaching people, what would you want Jesus explain to you or what would you ask Him do for you?

_____

_____

_____

_____

_____

➤ Why do you think people were excited to tell others about Jesus?

_____

_____

_____

_____

_____

➤ What do you think the people thought John the Baptist meant when he said, "I baptize you with water, but Jesus will baptize you with the Holy Spirit?"

_____

_____

_____

_____

_____

➤ What kinds of changes do you think people experience in their lives when Jesus baptizes them with the Holy Spirit?

_____

_____

_____

_____

_____

➤ Why do you think Jesus went out alone to pray before daylight, and how might praying alone, early in the morning, be helpful to you?

_____

_____

_____

_____

_____

➤ What moves you toward feeling compassion for other people?

_____

_____

_____

_____

_____

➤ From what sins might you need to repent? (Repenting is asking for forgiveness and turning away from that sin.)

_____

_____

_____

_____

_____

➤ What do you think you need to know or do to be able to follow Jesus spiritually?

_____

_____

_____

_____

_____

➤ Jesus responded to anyone who asked for His help, no matter who they were. What kinds of things does Jesus' example teach us about helping people?

_____

_____

_____

_____

_____

_____

ACTION ITEMS:

➤ Name some things you would like to do, do more, or do better, based on Jesus' examples so far:

_____

_____

_____

_____

_____

WHAT'S NEXT?

In the next chapter, the religious leaders of the day began to hear about and take notice of Jesus. They didn't like what Jesus was telling people. The religious leaders also didn't like the sorts of people Jesus dined with, so the leaders began trying to discredit Jesus. As you read the next chapter, notice how the controversy between Jesus and church officials begins to develop.

2 CONTROVERSY STIRS

When he entered again into Capernaum after some days, it was heard that he was in the house. Immediately many were gathered together, so that there was no more room, not even around the door; and he spoke the word to them. Four people came, carrying a paralytic to him. When they could not come near to him for the crowd, they removed the roof where he was. When they had broken it up, they let down the mat that the paralytic was lying on. Jesus, seeing their faith, said to the paralytic, *"Son, your sins are forgiven you."*

But there were some of the scribes sitting there, and reasoning in their hearts, "Why does this man speak blasphemies like that? Who can forgive sins but God alone?"

Immediately Jesus, perceiving in his spirit that they so reasoned within themselves, said to them, *"Why do you reason these things in your hearts? Which is easier, to tell the paralytic, 'Your sins are forgiven;' or to say, 'Arise, and take up your bed, and walk?' But that you may know that the Son of Man has authority on earth to forgive sins"*—he said to the paralytic— *"I tell you, arise, take up your mat, and go to your house."*

He arose, and immediately took up the mat, and went out in front of them all; so that they were all amazed, and glorified God, saying, "We never saw anything like this!" He went out again by the seaside. All the multitude came to him, and he taught them. As he passed by, he saw Levi, the son of Alphaeus, sitting at the tax office, and he said to him, *"Follow me."* And he arose and followed him.

He was reclining at the table in his house, and many tax collectors and sinners sat down with Jesus and his disciples, for there were many, and they followed him. The scribes and the Pharisees, when they saw that he was eating with the sinners and tax collectors, said to his disciples, "Why is it that he eats and drinks with tax collectors and sinners?"

When Jesus heard it, he said to them, *"Those who are healthy have no need for a physician, but those who are sick. I came not to call the righteous, but sinners to repentance."*

John's disciples and the Pharisees were fasting, and they came and asked him,

"Why do John's disciples and the disciples of the Pharisees fast, but your disciples don't fast?"

Jesus said to them, *"Can the groomsmen fast while the bridegroom is with them? As long as they have the bridegroom with them, they can't fast. But the days will come when the bridegroom will be taken away from them, and then they will fast in that day. No one sews a piece of unshrunk cloth on an old garment, or else the patch shrinks and the new tears away from the old, and a worse hole is made. No one puts new wine into old wineskins, or else the new wine will burst the skins, and the wine pours out, and the skins will be destroyed; but they put new wine into fresh wineskins."*

He was going on the Sabbath day through the grain fields, and his disciples began, as they went, to pluck the ears of grain. The Pharisees said to him, "Behold, why do they do that which is not lawful on the Sabbath day?"

He said to them, *"Did you never read what David did, when he had need, and was hungry—he, and those who were with him? How he entered into God's house at the time of Abiathar the high priest, and ate the show bread, which is not lawful to eat except for the priests, and gave also to those who were with him?"* He said to them, *"The Sabbath was made for man, not man for the Sabbath. Therefore the Son of Man is lord even of the Sabbath."*

DID YOU NOTICE?

Chapter 2 starts with Jesus traveling to Capernaum. Huge crowds gather to hear Jesus. There are so many people, no one can get into the house where Jesus is staying.

In this chapter we see the first accusations against Jesus by church members. They accuse Him of blasphemy because He told the paralytic, *"Your sins are forgiven."*

When the church members start grumbling, Jesus says he will prove He has authority to forgive sins by doing something harder. Jesus heals the paralytic on the spot. The people are amazed, and Jesus' fame spread. Multitudes of people start coming to see Jesus.

At the close of this chapter, Jesus reclines with unsavory people by the self-righteous church members' standards. It's appalling to them that Jesus visits with sinners and tax collectors.

Jesus was seemingly an ordinary guy who was spending time with ordinary people. Jesus wasn't trying to impress the religious leaders.

➤ Tensions begin to mount between Jesus and religious leaders, because Jesus spoke with authority about religious matters. The bottom line is: religious leaders didn't like Jesus. Are they jealous? Do they think they know more than Jesus? Why do you think they don't like Jesus, especially when the crowds love Him?

_____

_____

_____

_____

_____

WHAT DO YOU THINK?

➤ Picture yourself with Jesus. Would you be amazed and want to hear more from Jesus? Or would you be sneering and wondering, "Who does Jesus think He is talking like He has authority over everybody and everything, even forgiving sins?" Describe how you think you would react to Jesus:

_____

_____

_____

_____

_____

➤ Why do you think the religious leaders were angry Jesus forgave a man's sins?

_____

_____

_____

_____

_____

_____

➤ How would you feel if you met Jesus today, and He told you all of your sins are forgiven? What difference do you think it'd make to you spiritually?

_____

_____

_____

_____

_____

_____

➤ Jesus saw the faith of the paralytic and his friends. In response to their faith, Jesus said, "*Your sins are forgiven.*" What do you think this story implies you need to do or have for your sins to be forgiven?

_____

_____

_____

_____

_____

➤ For what sins in your life do you especially want God to forgive you?

_____

_____

_____

_____

_____

➢ Since Jesus said He came to heal sinners, describe the kinds of people you would expect Jesus to seek to talk to:

_____

_____

_____

_____

_____

➢ Do you think the religious leaders thought Jesus was a saint or a sinner? Why?

_____

_____

_____

_____

_____

➢ Based on the verses about fasting, what purpose do you think fasting might serve?

_____

_____

_____

_____

_____

➢ What do you think Jesus means when He says, *"The Sabbath was made for man, not man for the Sabbath?"*

_____

_____

_____

_____

_____

_____

➢ In who or what does Jesus want us to have faith? Why is it good to have faith?

_____

_____

_____

_____

_____

➢ So far, do you like Jesus? Why or why not?

_____

_____

_____

_____

_____

_____

ACTION ITEM:

☐ Ask God to forgive all of your sins.

WHAT'S NEXT?

Look for the religious leaders to start conspiring against Jesus. Put yourself in the room with Jesus and decide for yourself: What is the nature of Jesus' ministry to the common people? And why are the religious leaders so zealous against Jesus?

3 IS JESUS GOOD OR EVIL?

He entered again into the synagogue, and there was a man there who had his hand withered. They watched him, whether he would heal him on the Sabbath day, that they might accuse him. He said to the man who had his hand withered, *"Stand up."* He said to them, *"Is it lawful on the Sabbath day to do good, or to do harm? To save a life, or to kill?"* But they were silent. When he had looked around at them with anger, being grieved at the hardening of their hearts, he said to the man, *"Stretch out your hand."* He stretched it out, and his hand was restored as healthy as the other. The Pharisees went out, and immediately conspired with the Herodians against him, how they might destroy him.

Jesus withdrew to the sea with his disciples, and a great multitude followed him from Galilee, from Judea, from Jerusalem, from Idumaea, beyond the

Jordan, and those from around Tyre and Sidon. A great multitude, hearing what great things he did, came to him. He spoke to his disciples that a little boat should stay near him because of the crowd, so that they wouldn't press on him.

For he had healed many, so that as many as had diseases pressed on him that they might touch him. The unclean spirits, whenever they saw him, fell down before him, and cried, "You are the Son of God!" He sternly warned them that they should not make him known.

He went up into the mountain, and called to himself those whom he wanted, and they went to him. He appointed twelve, that they might be with him, and that he might send them out to preach, and to have authority to heal sicknesses and to cast out demons: Simon (to whom he gave the name Peter); James the son of Zebedee; and John, the brother of James, (whom he called Boanerges, which means, Sons of Thunder); Andrew; Philip; Bartholomew; Matthew; Thomas; James, the son of Alphaeus; Thaddaeus; Simon the Zealot; and Judas Iscariot, who also betrayed him.

Then he came into a house. The multitude came together again, so that they could not so much as eat bread. When his friends heard it, they went out to seize him; for they said, "He is insane." The scribes who came down from Jerusalem said, "He has Beelzebul," and, "By the prince of the demons he casts out the demons."

He summoned them, and said to them in parables, *"How can Satan cast out Satan? If a kingdom is divided against itself, that kingdom cannot stand. If a house is divided against itself, that house cannot stand. If Satan has risen up against himself, and is divided, he can't stand, but has an end. But no one can enter into the house of the strong man to plunder unless he first binds the strong man; then he will plunder his house. Most certainly I tell you, all sins of the descendants of man will be forgiven, including their blasphemies with which they may blaspheme; but whoever may blaspheme against the Holy Spirit never has forgiveness, but is subject to eternal condemnation."* — because they said, "He has an unclean spirit."

His mother and his brothers came, and standing outside, they sent to him, calling him. A multitude was sitting around him, and they told him, "Behold, your mother, your brothers, and your sisters are outside looking for you."

He answered them, *"Who are my mother and my brothers?"* Looking around at those who sat around him, he said, *"Behold, my mother and my brothers! For whoever does the will of God is my brother, my sister, and mother."*

DID YOU NOTICE?

At the opening of chapter three, the church leaders are looking for a way to discredit Jesus. They're watching him carefully, and the Pharisees begin conspiring to destroy Jesus. After all, Jesus healed a man and the Pharisees didn't approve!

In this chapter, we also see the crowds are huge, and they follow Jesus everywhere He goes. We'll see the crowds grow in the coming chapters as the news about Jesus spreads.

Did you notice in this chapter Jesus selected twelve men from among those who were following Him? Jesus selected these twelve disciples so He could teach and mentor them until His death. These men continued teaching all they learned from Jesus after He died. Some of them also wrote books which became part of the Bible.

Lastly, in chapter 3, did you notice the religious leaders saying Jesus has a demon, and some of Jesus' family thought He had lost his mind?

Jesus clearly explained, He can't be serving Satan or demons, if He is casting demons out. Jesus is serving God by going against Satan.

➢ Jesus' family members think He's crazy and may be embarrassed by His teaching. However, Jesus teaches a new concept—His family consists of people who do God's will. What do you think Jesus' family members thought about this teaching?

_____

_____

_____

_____

_____

_____

_____

WHAT DO YOU THINK?

➢ Why do you think the religious scribes believe Jesus is serving demons?

_____

_____

_____

_____

_____

➢ Do you think Jesus is crazy or possessed by a demon? Why or why not?

_____

_____

_____

_____

_____

_____

➢ Would you consider Jesus' deeds and actions to be good or evil? Why?

_____

_____

_____

_____

_____

_____

➢ Why do you think Jesus' family members think He is crazy or has lost His mind?

_____

_____

_____

_____

_____

➢ Based on what Jesus says, what kinds of things is it okay to do on the Sabbath?

_____

_____

_____

_____

_____

➤ At this point in the book, what do you think attracted so many people to Jesus?

_____

_____

_____

_____

_____

_____

_____

➤ What do you think the crowds would be like if Jesus came to your town today?

_____

_____

_____

_____

_____

_____

_____

➤ If Jesus came to your town today, what would you like Jesus to heal in you?

_____

_____

_____

_____

_____

➤ List character traits you think the 12 disciples needed for Jesus to pick them as His students. Circle the character traits you think you have.

_____

_____

_____

_____

_____

_____

➤ Jesus says a house or a kingdom divided against itself cannot stand. What happens to families when they are divided and argue a lot?

_____

_____

_____

_____

_____

_____

➤ What are some ways people create divisions within their own families?

_____

_____

_____

_____

_____

_____

ACTION ITEM:

➤ Name some things you can do to strengthen your family bonds:

_____

_____

_____

_____

_____

_____

_____

(If you want to know more about the will of God, read God's commands in the Bible. You can find the most important ones in your Bible in Exodus chapter 20, Matthew chapter 22 - verses 35-40, and in the book of Matthew in chapters 5-7.)

WHAT'S NEXT?

In the next chapter, Jesus begins teaching the crowds with parables. In the Bible, in chapter 13 of the book of Matthew, the disciples directly ask Jesus WHY He teaches in parables. Matthew 13:10-16 says:

The disciples came, and said to him, "Why do you speak to them in parables?"

He answered them, "*To you it is given to know the mysteries of the Kingdom of Heaven, but it is not given to them. For whoever has, to him will be given, and he will have abundance; but whoever doesn't have, from him will be taken away even that which he has. Therefore I speak to them in parables, because seeing they don't see, and hearing, they don't hear, neither do they understand. In them the prophecy of Isaiah is fulfilled, which says,*

'By hearing you will hear,

and will in no way understand;

Seeing you will see,

and will in no way perceive;

for this people's heart has grown callous,

their ears are dull of hearing,

and they have closed their eyes;

or else perhaps they might perceive with their eyes,

hear with their ears,

understand with their heart,

and would turn again,

and I would heal them.' (Isaiah 6:9-10)

"But blessed are your eyes, for they see; and your ears, for they hear."

As you read the next chapter, pay close attention to the story. Whisper a request to God to help you understand Jesus' parables! See if you can understand it as you read.

4 JESUS SOWS SEEDS

Again he began to teach by the seaside. A great multitude was gathered to him, so that he entered into a boat in the sea, and sat down. All the multitude were on the land by the sea.

He taught them many things in parables, and told them in his teaching, *"Listen! Behold, the farmer went out to sow, and as he sowed, some seed fell by the road, and the birds came and devoured it. Others fell on the rocky ground, where it had little soil, and immediately it sprang up, because it had no depth of soil. When the sun had risen, it was scorched; and because it had no root, it withered away. Others fell among the thorns, and the thorns grew up, and choked it, and it yielded no fruit. Others fell into the good ground, and yielded fruit, growing up and increasing. Some produced thirty* _times, some sixty times, and some one hundred times as much."_ He said, _"Whoever has ears to hear, let him hear."_

When he was alone, those who were around him with the twelve asked him about the parables. He said to them, _"To you is given the mystery of God's Kingdom, but to those who are outside, all things are done in parables, that 'seeing they may see, and not perceive; and hearing they may hear, and not understand; lest perhaps they should turn again, and their sins should be forgiven them.'"_

He said to them, _"Don't you understand this parable? How will you understand all of the parables? The farmer sows the word. The ones by the road are the ones where the word is sown; and when they have heard, immediately Satan comes, and takes away the word which has been sown in them. These in the same way are those who are sown on the rocky places, who, when they have heard the word, immediately receive it with joy. They have no root in themselves, but are short-lived. When oppression or persecution arises because of the word, immediately they stumble. Others are those who are sown among the thorns. These are those who have heard the word, and the cares of this age, and the deceitfulness of riches, and the lusts of other things entering in choke the word, and it becomes unfruitful._

"Those which were sown on the good ground are those who hear the word, and accept it, and bear fruit, some thirty times, some sixty times, and some one hundred times."

He said to them, "Is the lamp brought to be put under a basket or under a bed? Isn't it put on a stand? For there is nothing hidden, except that it should be made known; neither was anything made secret, but that it should come to light. If any man has ears to hear, let him hear."

He said to them, "Take heed what you hear. With whatever measure you measure, it will be measured to you, and more will be given to you who hear. For whoever has, to him more will be given, and he who doesn't have, even that which he has will be taken away from him."

He said, "God's Kingdom is as if a man should cast seed on the earth, and should sleep and rise night and day, and the seed should spring up and grow, though he doesn't know how. For the earth bears fruit: first the blade, then the ear, then the full grain in the ear. But when the fruit is ripe, immediately he puts in the sickle, because the harvest has come."

He said, "How will we liken God's Kingdom? Or with what parable will we illustrate it? It's like a grain of mustard seed, which, when it is sown in the earth, though it is less than all the seeds *that are on the earth, yet when it is sown, grows up, and becomes greater than all the herbs, and puts out great branches, so that the birds of the sky can lodge under its shadow."*

With many such parables he spoke the word to them, as they were able to hear it. Without a parable he didn't speak to them; but privately to his own disciples he explained everything.

On that day, when evening had come, he said to them, *"Let's go over to the other side."* Leaving the multitude, they took him with them, even as he was, in the boat. Other small boats were also with him.

A big wind storm arose, and the waves beat into the boat, so much that the boat was already filled. He himself was in the stern, asleep on the cushion, and they woke him up, and told him, "Teacher, don't you care that we are dying?"

He awoke, and rebuked the wind, and said to the sea, *"Peace! Be still!"*

The wind ceased, and there was a great calm. He said to them, *"Why are you so afraid? How is it that you have no faith?"*

They were greatly afraid, and said to one another, "Who then is this, that even the wind and the sea obey him?"

DID YOU NOTICE?

Did you notice that Jesus' teachings are not as easy to understand in this chapter? He is beginning to teach in parables, and His teachings are more obscure for a reason.

When people hear the word of God, one of four things happen:

1. Nothing—the person doesn't connect with God's Word at all. The person's mind and heart dismiss what is said, and God's Word never takes root.

2. The person is excited, but the excitement wears off quickly. In this case, the person likes what he hears, but doesn't really take the Word into his heart. Within a short period of time, the initial excitement disappears, and God's Word has no effect on the person's life going forward.

3. The person's mind and heart connect with God's Word. This person is excited and has the best intentions for putting the information to good use in his life. Unfortunately, daily life gets in the way, and God's Word is put on the "do later" list. Nothing productive comes from hearing God's Word, because it is not adopted and acted upon.

4. The fourth type of person latches on to God's Word. The person pursues a deeper understanding of God and His will. This person becomes fruitful in producing great changes in his life, through God's guidance, grace, and gifting.

Jesus stresses, *"Whoever has ears, let him hear."* He also says there is nothing hidden or secret which won't come to be known or understood. The key is to truly listen to Jesus with your heart and mind. You have to seek to understand the mysteries of God's Kingdom. If we seek to know God, His ways and His Kingdom will be revealed to us.

When verses talk about getting out whatever measure you put in, it means you will gain from whatever effort you put into understanding Jesus' teachings. If you pursue understanding God and Jesus with a passion, you will grow with the amount of effort you put in. If you skim His Word, and put little effort into understanding what Jesus is teaching, you will get little out of it.

In other words, God will help you grow your seeds, whether you sow sparingly or with a generous measure. The key to growing your harvest: You have to nurture your seeds. You have to put forth effort and make it a priority to understand God.

➢ What are some things you could do regularly to improve your spiritual soil and grow in your relationship with God?

_____

_____

_____

_____

_____

_____

_____

_____

WHAT DO YOU THINK?

➢ Why do you think God wants people to seek to understand Him and His Kingdom?

_____

_____

_____

_____

_____

_____

_____

_____

_____

➢ By reading this study, you are sowing seeds. What kind of results do you hope to gain by learning more about God and Jesus?

_____

_____

_____

_____

_____

_____

_____

_____

_____

_____

➤ Of the four outcomes from scattering seed (roadside, rocky ground, shallow ground, or rich soil), which do you think is most common and why?

_____

_____

_____

_____

➤ Jesus talks about the mystery of the kingdom of God. What do you find mysterious about God's Kingdom?

_____

_____

_____

_____

➤ If you don't understand Jesus' Parables, what are some steps can you take to find out what His parables mean?

_____

_____

_____

_____

➤ If nothing will be hidden, everything is revealed, and all secrets are known, what past actions might you need to make amends for while you can?

_____

_____

_____

_____

_____

➢ In what ways is God's kingdom like growing a harvest from seeds or growing a mustard seed? (Look up information about growing mustard seeds and mustard plants, if it might help you answer this question.)

_____

_____

_____

_____

_____

➢ In what way do you think your fears show the strength or weakness of your faith?

_____

_____

_____

_____

_____

➢ What do you think Jesus wants us to do when we feel fearful?

_____

_____

_____

_____

_____

ACTION ITEM:

Pray for wisdom and insight to understand God's Mysteries.

WHAT'S NEXT?

Jesus performs dramatic miracles in the next chapter, which impact the lives of everyone who witnesses the miracles. Symbolically speaking, see which of the healing miracles you can relate to the most.

5 THREE MAJOR MIRACLES

They came to the other side of the sea, into the country of the Gadarenes. When he had come out of the boat, immediately a man with an unclean spirit met him out of the tombs. He lived in the tombs. Nobody could bind him anymore, not even with chains, because he had been often bound with fetters and chains, and the chains had been torn apart by him, and the fetters broken in pieces. Nobody had the strength to tame him. Always, night and day, in the tombs and in the mountains, he was crying out, and cutting himself with stones. When he saw Jesus from afar, he ran and bowed down to him, and crying out with a loud voice, he said, "What have I to do with you, Jesus, you Son of the Most High God? I adjure you by God, don't torment me."

For he said to him, *"Come out of the man, you unclean spirit!"*

Jesus asked him, *"What is your name?"*

He said to Jesus, "My name is Legion, for we are many." He begged him much that he would not send them away out of the country. Now on the mountainside there was a great herd of pigs feeding. All the demons begged him, saying, "Send us into the pigs, that we may enter into them."

At once Jesus gave them permission. The unclean spirits came out and entered into the pigs. The herd of about two thousand rushed down the steep bank into the sea, and they were drowned in the sea. Those who fed them fled, and told it in the city and in the country.

The people came to see what it was that had happened. They came to Jesus, and saw him who had been possessed by demons sitting, clothed, and in his right mind, even him who had the legion; and they were afraid. Those who saw it declared to them what happened to him who was possessed by demons, and about the pigs. They began to beg him to depart from their region.

As he was entering into the boat, he who had been possessed by demons begged him that he might be with him. He didn't allow him, but said to him, *"Go to your house, to your friends, and tell them what great things the Lord has done for you, and how he had mercy on you."*

He went his way, and began to proclaim in Decapolis how Jesus had done great things for him, and everyone marveled.

When Jesus had crossed back over in the boat to the other side, a great multitude was gathered to him; and he was by the sea. Behold, one of the rulers of the synagogue, Jairus by name, came; and seeing him, he fell at his feet, and begged him much, saying, "My little daughter is at the point of death. Please come and lay your hands on her, that she may be made healthy, and live."

He went with him, and a great multitude followed him, and they pressed upon him on all sides. A certain woman, who had a discharge of blood for twelve years, and had suffered many things by many physicians, and had spent all that she had, and was no better, but rather grew worse, having heard the things concerning Jesus, came up behind him in the crowd, and touched his clothes. For she said, "If I just touch his clothes, I will be made well." Immediately the flow of her blood was dried up, and she felt in her body that she was healed of her affliction.

Immediately Jesus, perceiving in himself that the power had gone out from him, turned around in the crowd, and asked, *"Who touched my clothes?"*

His disciples said to him, "You see the multitude pressing against you, and you say, 'Who touched me?'"

He looked around to see her who had done this thing. But the woman, fearing and trembling, knowing what had been done to her, came and fell down before him, and told him all the truth.

He said to her, *"Daughter, your faith has made you well. Go in peace, and be cured of your disease."*

While he was still speaking, people came from the synagogue ruler's house saying, "Your daughter is dead. Why bother the Teacher anymore?"

But Jesus, when he heard the message spoken, immediately said to the ruler of the synagogue, *"Don't be afraid, only believe."*

He allowed no one to follow him, except Peter, James, and John the brother of James. He came to the synagogue ruler's house, and he saw an uproar, weeping, and great wailing. When he had entered in, he said to them, *"Why do you make an uproar and weep? The child is not dead, but is asleep."*

They ridiculed him. But he, having put them all out, took the father of the child, her mother, and those who were with him, and went in where the child was lying. Taking the child by the hand, he said to her, *"Talitha cumi!"* which means, being interpreted, *"Girl, I tell you, get up!"* Immediately the girl rose up and walked, for she was twelve years old. They were amazed with great amazement.

He strictly ordered them that no one should know this, and commanded that something should be given to her to eat.

DID YOU NOTICE?

There are three major miracles in this chapter, showing what Jesus is capable of doing. Did you notice the role FAITH played in these miracles and Jesus told people their faith was a key to the success of the miracle? If faith affects your ability to experience miracles, how might your current level of faith affect your ability to experience miracles in your life?

_____

_____

_____

_____

_____

_____

_____

WHAT DO YOU THINK?

➤ If Jesus was in front of you at this moment, what is the biggest miracle you would want him to perform in your life?

_____

_____

_____

_____

_____

_____

➤ How would you celebrate if Jesus performed the miracle you most desire?

_____

_____

_____

_____

_____

_____

_____

➤ Who would you want to tell about the miracle and, what would you hope their reaction would be toward you and Jesus?

_____

_____

_____

_____

_____

_____

➤ From Jesus' words about faith and miracles, why do you think most people don't experience miracles in today's world?

_____

_____

_____

_____

_____

_____

_____

➤ If you don't think your faith in God is strong enough to witness miracles, how might you overcome your doubts and strengthen your faith?

_____

_____

_____

_____

_____

➤ What problems and issues keep you from living your life with joy and zeal?

_____

_____

_____

_____

_____

➢ What "bindings" do you feel are holding you back in life? If Jesus is all powerful, and He can break any binding, from what binding would you ask Jesus to break you free?

_____

_____

_____

_____

_____

_____

➢ Why is it difficult for us to have unwavering faith and to believe God can do anything?

_____

_____

_____

_____

_____

_____

ACTION ITEM:

Sincerely pray for God to strengthen your faith, and for any miracles you desire.

WHAT'S NEXT?

In the next chapter, observe what happens when people have doubts rather than faith. What happens to the miracles Jesus tries to perform in the next chapter? See if you can figure out why King Herod is so afraid of John the Baptist, even though King Herod had John beheaded.

6 DOUBT, FEAR, AND FAITH

Jesus went out from there. He came into his own country, and his disciples followed him. When the Sabbath had come, he began to teach in the synagogue, and many hearing him were astonished, saying, "Where did this man get these things?" and, "What is the wisdom that is given to this man, that such mighty works come about by his hands? Isn't this the carpenter, the son of Mary, and brother of James, Joses, Judah, and Simon? Aren't his sisters here with us?" They were offended at him.

Jesus said to them, *"A prophet is not without honor, except in his own country, and among his own relatives, and in his own house."* He could do no mighty work there, except that he laid his hands on a few sick people, and healed them.

He marveled because of their unbelief.

Jesus went around the villages teaching. He called to himself the twelve, and began to send them out two by two; and he gave them authority over the unclean spirits. He commanded them that they should take nothing for their journey, except a staff only: no bread, no wallet, and no money in their purse, but to wear sandals, and not put on two tunics. He said to them, *"Wherever you enter into a house, stay there until you depart from there. Whoever will not receive you nor hear you, as you depart from there, shake off the dust that is under your feet for a testimony against them. Assuredly, I tell you, it will be more tolerable for Sodom and Gomorrah in the day of judgment than for that city!"*

They went out and preached that people should repent. They cast out many demons, and anointed many with oil who were sick, and healed them.

King Herod heard this, for his name had become known, and he said, "John the Baptizer has risen from the dead, and therefore these powers are at work in him." But others said, "He is Elijah." Others said, "He is a prophet, or like one of the prophets." But Herod, when he heard this, said, "This is John, whom I beheaded. He has risen from the dead." For Herod himself had sent out and arrested John, and bound him in prison for the sake of Herodias, his brother Philip's wife, for he had married her.

For John said to Herod, "It is not

lawful for you to have your brother's wife." Herodias set herself against him, and desired to kill him, but she couldn't, for Herod feared John, knowing that he was a righteous and holy man, and kept him safe. When he heard him, he did many things, and he heard him gladly.

Then a convenient day came, that Herod on his birthday made a supper for his nobles, the high officers, and the chief men of Galilee. When the daughter of Herodias herself came in and danced, she pleased Herod and those sitting with him. The king said to the young lady, "Ask me whatever you want, and I will give it to you." He swore to her, "Whatever you shall ask of me, I will give you, up to half of my kingdom."

She went out, and said to her mother, "What shall I ask?"

She said, "The head of John the Baptizer."

She came in immediately with haste to the king, and asked, "I want you to give me right now the head of John the Baptizer on a platter."

The king was exceedingly sorry, but for the sake of his oaths, and of his dinner guests, he didn't wish to refuse her. Immediately the king sent out a soldier of his guard, and commanded to bring John's head, and he went and beheaded him in the prison, and brought his head on a platter, and gave it to the young lady; and the young lady gave it to her mother.

When his disciples heard this, they came and took up his corpse, and laid it in a tomb.

The apostles gathered themselves together to Jesus, and they told him all things, whatever they had done, and whatever they had taught. He said to them, *"You come apart into a deserted place, and rest awhile."* For there were many coming and going, and they had no leisure so much as to eat. They went away in the boat to a deserted place by themselves. They saw them going, and many recognized him and ran there on foot from all the cities. They arrived before them and came together to him. Jesus came out, saw a great multitude, and he had compassion on them, because they were like sheep without a shepherd, and he began to teach them many things. When it was late in the day, his disciples came to him, and said, "This place is deserted, and it is late in the day. Send them away, that they may go into the surrounding country and villages, and buy themselves bread, for they have nothing to eat."

But he answered them, *"You give them something to eat."*

They asked him, "Shall we go and buy two hundred denarii worth of bread, and give them something to eat?"

He said to them, *"How many loaves do you have? Go see."*

When they knew, they said, "Five, and two fish."

He commanded them that everyone should sit down in groups on the green grass. They sat down in ranks, by hundreds and by fifties. He took the five loaves and the two fish, and looking up to heaven, he blessed and broke the loaves, and he gave to his disciples to set before them, and he divided the two fish among them all. They all ate, and were filled. They took up twelve baskets full of broken pieces and also of the fish. Those who ate the loaves were five thousand men.

Immediately he made his disciples get into the boat, and to go ahead to the other side, to Bethsaida, while he himself sent the multitude away. After he had taken leave of them, he went up the mountain to pray.

When evening had come, the boat was in the middle of the sea, and he was alone on the land. Seeing them distressed in rowing, for the wind was contrary to them, about the fourth watch of the night he came to them, walking on the sea, and he would have passed by them, but they, when they saw him walking on the sea, supposed that it was a ghost, and cried out; for they all saw him, and were troubled. But he immediately spoke with them, and said to them, *"Cheer up! It is I! Don't be afraid."* He got into the boat with them; and the wind ceased, and they were very amazed among themselves, and marveled; for they hadn't understood about the loaves, but their hearts were hardened.

When they had crossed over, they came to land at Gennesaret, and moored to the shore. When they had come out of the boat, immediately the people recognized him, and ran around that whole region, and began to bring those

_____

_____

_____

_____

_____

_____

_____

who were sick, on their mats, to where they heard he was. Wherever he entered, into villages, or into cities, or into the country, they laid the sick in the marketplaces, and begged him that they might just touch the fringe of his garment; and as many as touched him were made well.

DID YOU NOTICE?

Did you notice that Jesus couldn't perform as many miracles for his unbelieving family and townspeople? This concept is taught several times in the New Testament of the Bible: when people have faith in God they're more likely to experience miracles in their lives.

In this chapter, we also learned that King Herod thought Jesus was John the Baptist resurrected from the dead. Did you notice who other people thought Jesus might be? Describe who you think or believe Jesus is at this point:

_____

_____

_____

_____

_____

_____

_____

_____

WHAT DO YOU THINK?

➢ What surprises you the most about Jesus's teachings?

_____

_____

_____

_____

_____

_____

➢ The people from Jesus' town were offended by Jesus' wisdom. Why are family and friends more judgmental and critical of us than people we've just met?

_____

_____

_____

_____

_____

➢ King Herod felt condemned by his own guilty conscience. What makes you feel guilty when you've done something wrong? What emotions do you feel?

_____

_____

_____

_____

_____

➢ People usually know right from wrong, even when they aren't religious. Where do you think this inner knowledge of right and wrong comes from, when it isn't always learned through observation and/or direct instruction from our parents?

_____

_____

_____

_____

_____

➢ On a scale of 1 = NO Faith to 10 = TOTAL Faith, how strong is your faith that miracles actually happen? What would you say affects your level of faith?

_____

_____

_____

_____

_____

➤ Faith and belief allowed Jesus to perform miracles in chapter five. In this chapter, unbelief meant Jesus could do no miracles. How do these two outcomes shape your awareness of your faith, as you consider the outcomes for which you are hopeful?

_____

_____

_____

_____

_____

_____

➤ When we sin, why should we repent? What does repenting actually accomplish?

_____

_____

_____

_____

_____

_____

➤ What do you think happens in our souls when we go off by ourselves to rest and pray, as was Jesus' practice?

_____

_____

_____

_____

_____

➤ What kinds of circumstances move you toward compassion for other people?

_____

_____

_____

_____

_____

> If Jesus came to you walking on water, what kinds of thoughts would be running through your mind?

_____

_____

_____

_____

_____

_____

ACTION ITEM:

Ask God to increase your compassion for others, particularly for your family.

WHAT'S NEXT?

In the next chapter, notice the Pharisees travel to see Jesus. They condemn Jesus and His disciples. Also notice how a woman answers Jesus with faith and wisdom, so Jesus grants her request.

7 YOUR SOUL INSIDE AND OUT

Then the Pharisees and some of the scribes gathered together to him, having come from Jerusalem. Now when they saw some of his disciples eating bread with defiled, that is unwashed, hands, they found fault. (For the Pharisees and all the Jews don't eat unless they wash their hands and forearms, holding to the tradition of the elders. They don't eat when they come from the marketplace unless they bathe themselves, and there are many other things, which they have received to hold to: washings of cups, pitchers, bronze vessels, and couches.) The Pharisees and the scribes asked him, "Why don't your disciples walk according to the tradition of the elders, but eat their bread with unwashed hands?"

He answered them, *"Well did Isaiah prophesy of you hypocrites, as it is written, 'This people honors me with*

their lips, but their heart is far from me. But they worship me in vain, teaching as doctrines the commandments of men.'
"For you set aside the commandment of God, and hold tightly to the tradition of men—the washing of pitchers and cups, and you do many other such things."

He said to them, *"Full well do you reject the commandment of God, that you may keep your tradition. For Moses said, 'Honor your father and your mother;' and, 'He who speaks evil of father or mother, let him be put to death.' But you say, 'If a man tells his father or his mother, "Whatever profit you might have received from me is Corban,' that is to say, given to God, then you no longer allow him to do anything for his father or his mother, making void the word of God by your tradition, which you have handed down. You do many things like this."*

He called all the multitude to himself, and said to them, *"Hear me, all of you, and understand. There is nothing from outside of the man, that going into him can defile him; but the things which proceed out of the man are those that defile the man. If anyone has ears to hear, let him hear!"*

When he had entered into a house away from the multitude, his disciples asked him about the parable. He said to them, *"Are you also without understanding? Don't you perceive that whatever goes into the man from outside can't defile him, because it doesn't go into his heart, but into his stomach, then into the latrine, making all foods clean?"* He said, *"That which proceeds out of the man, that defiles the man. For from within, out of the hearts of men, proceed evil thoughts, adulteries, sexual sins, murders, thefts, coveting, wickedness, deceit, lustful desires, an evil eye, blasphemy, pride, and foolishness. All these evil things come from within, and defile the man."*

From there he arose, and went away into the borders of Tyre and Sidon. He entered into a house, and didn't want anyone to know it, but he couldn't escape notice. For a woman, whose little daughter had an unclean spirit, having heard of him, came and fell down at his feet. Now the woman was a Greek, a Syrophoenician by race. She begged him that he would cast the demon out of her daughter. But Jesus said to her, *"Let the children be filled first, for it is not appropriate to take the children's bread and throw it to the dogs."*

But she answered him, "Yes, Lord. Yet even the dogs under the table eat the children's crumbs."

He said to her, *"For this saying, go your way. The demon has gone out of your daughter."*

She went away to her house, and found the child having been laid on the bed, with the demon gone out.

Again he departed from the borders of Tyre and Sidon, and came to the Sea of Galilee, through the middle of the region

_____

_____

_____

_____

_____

_____

_____

_____

_____

_____

_____

_____

_____

_____

_____

of Decapolis. They brought to him one who was deaf and had an impediment in his speech. They begged him to lay his hand on him. He took him aside from the multitude, privately, and put his fingers into his ears, and he spat, and touched his tongue. Looking up to heaven, he sighed, and said to him, *"Ephphatha!"* that is, *"Be opened!"* Immediately his ears were opened, and the impediment of his tongue was released, and he spoke clearly. He commanded them that they should tell no one, but the more he commanded them, so much the more widely they proclaimed it. They were astonished beyond measure, saying, "He has done all things well. He makes even the deaf hear, and the mute speak!"

DID YOU NOTICE?

The Pharisees were trying to condemn Jesus, but Jesus used the opportunity to point out the Pharisees' sins. The Pharisees saw themselves as righteous and upstanding, even though they failed to keep God's commandments in favor of their own rules. Do you see similarities between the Pharisees' judgment of others and how people judge others today?

Another important teaching of Jesus in this chapter relates to what defiles a person. Defiling is defined as spoiling, ruining, desecrating, or violating. Jesus makes it clear what a person eats doesn't ruin a person's soul. On the other hand, what comes out of a person's heart or mind can ruin a person's soul.

Think about what really defiles a soul. For instance, can drugs or alcohol ruin a person's soul by itself, or is it the person's actions while under the influence that reveal the true state of the person's heart and mind? What are your thoughts?

_____

_____

_____

_____

_____

WHAT DO YOU THINK?

➢ What is the difference between consuming something that harms your body versus taking in something that defiles your soul?

_____

_____

_____

_____

_____

➢ What kinds of harmful or hurtful thoughts and actions come out of you toward other people?

_____

_____

_____

_____

_____

➢ What comes out of you, your mind, and heart that brings good into the world, or what comes out of you that is good?

_____

_____

_____

_____

_____

➢ What is the biggest sin coming out of you, and what can you do to stop the sin?

_____

_____

_____

_____

_____

➢ Why do people like to establish traditions, and what benefit(s) do we get from having traditions?

_____

_____

_____

_____

_____

_____

_____

➢ Why is it important to know more about God's Commandments than church traditions?

_____

_____

_____

_____

_____

_____

_____

➢ How can you be sure your church's traditions are aligned with God's actual Commandments?

_____

_____

_____

_____

_____

➢ Which of God's ten commandments do you know without looking them up?

_____

_____

_____

_____

_____

_____

_____

_____

_____

_____

_____

_____

_____

_____

➢ List a summary of God's Ten Commandments from Exodus 20. (You can go to: https://www.biblegateway.com/ and type Exodus 20 in the search box.)

_____

_____

_____

_____

_____

_____

_____

_____

_____

_____

_____

_____

_____

_____

_____

_____

_____

_____

➢ Why do you think people proclaimed Jesus' miracles even though He told them not to tell anyone?

_____

_____

_____

_____

_____

➢ If Jesus performed a miracle for you, who would you want to tell and why?

_____

_____

_____

_____

_____

➢ If Jesus performed a miracle for you, would you honestly be able to keep it a secret? Why or why not?

_____

_____

_____

_____

_____

ACTION ITEM:

Ask God to show you your sins and ask Him to help you overcome them.

WHAT'S NEXT?

In the next chapter, pay close attention to the cost of following Jesus. Ask yourself, "Why would people follow Jesus given the cost?"

8 BREAD SIGNS

In those days, when there was a very great multitude, and they had nothing to eat, Jesus called his disciples to himself, and said to them, *"I have compassion on the multitude, because they have stayed with me now three days, and have nothing to eat. If I send them away fasting to their home, they will faint on the way, for some of them have come a long way."*

His disciples answered him, "From where could one satisfy these people with bread here in a deserted place?"

He asked them, *"How many loaves do you have?"* They said, "Seven."

He commanded the multitude to sit down on the ground, and he took the seven loaves. Having given thanks, he broke them, and gave them to his disciples to serve, and they served the multitude. They had a few small fish.

Having blessed them, he said to serve these also. They ate, and were filled. They took up seven baskets of broken pieces that were left over. Those who had eaten were about four thousand. Then he sent them away.

Immediately he entered into the boat with his disciples, and came into the region of Dalmanutha. The Pharisees came out and began to question him, seeking from him a sign from heaven, and testing him. He sighed deeply in his spirit, and said, *"Why does this generation seek a sign? Most certainly I tell you, no sign will be given to this generation."*

He left them, and again entering into the boat, departed to the other side. They forgot to take bread; and they didn't have more than one loaf in the boat with them. He warned them, saying, *"Take heed: beware of the yeast of the Pharisees and the yeast of Herod."*

They reasoned with one another, saying, "It's because we have no bread."

Jesus, perceiving it, said to them, *"Why do you reason that it's because you have no bread? Don't you perceive yet, neither understand? Is your heart still hardened? Having eyes, don't you see? Having ears, don't you hear? Don't you remember? When I broke the five loaves among the five thousand, how many baskets full of broken pieces did you take up?"*

They told him, "Twelve."

"When the seven loaves fed the four

thousand, how many baskets full of broken pieces did you take up?"

They told him, "Seven."

He asked them, *"Don't you understand yet?"*

He came to Bethsaida. They brought a blind man to him, and begged him to touch him. He took hold of the blind man by the hand, and brought him out of the village. When he had spat on his eyes, and laid his hands on him, he asked him if he saw anything.

He looked up, and said, "I see men; for I see them like trees walking."

Then again he laid his hands on his eyes. He looked intently, and was restored, and saw everyone clearly. He sent him away to his house, saying, *"Don't enter into the village, nor tell anyone in the village."*

Jesus went out, with his disciples, into the villages of Caesarea Philippi. On the way he asked his disciples,

"Who do men say that I am?"

They told him, "John the Baptist, and others say Elijah, but others: one of the prophets."

He said to them, *"But who do you say that I am?"*

Peter answered, "You are the Christ."

He commanded them that they should tell no one about him. He began to teach them that the Son of Man must suffer many things, and be rejected by the elders, the chief priests, and the scribes, and be killed, and after three days rise again. He spoke to them openly.

Peter took him, and began to rebuke him. But he, turning around, and seeing his disciples, rebuked Peter, and said, *"Get behind me, Satan! For you have in mind not the things of God, but the things of men."*

He called the multitude to himself with his disciples, and said to them, *"Whoever wants to come after me, let him deny himself, and take up his cross, and follow me. For whoever wants to save his life will lose it; and whoever will lose his life for my sake and the sake of the Good News will save it. For what does it profit a man, to gain the whole world, and forfeit his life? For what will a man give in exchange for his life? For whoever will be ashamed of me and of my words in this adulterous and sinful generation, the Son of Man also will be ashamed of him, when he comes in his Father's glory, with the holy angels."*

DID YOU NOTICE?

Jesus sighed, as if he was exasperated, when the Pharisees asked Him for a sign. Jesus was performing miracles all over the place. Why do you think the Pharisees didn't see the signs that were right in front of them? Why do you think Jesus told them no other sign would be given to them?

Also, did you notice Jesus didn't explain what he meant when he said, *"Take heed: beware of the yeast of the Pharisees and the yeast of Herod."* Jesus responded to the disciple's confusion with a series of questions. Why do you think Jesus expected them to understand without further explanation?

_____

_____

_____

_____

_____

_____

_____

WHAT DO YOU THINK?

➢ If someone asked you at this point in the book of Mark, "Who would you say Jesus is?" what would be your answer?

_____

_____

_____

_____

_____

_____

_____

➢ What did Jesus tell the disciples about how He would die and what would happen after His death?

_____

_____

_____

_____

_____

_____

_____

➤ What does it mean for you to have the things of man in your mind, rather than the things of God?

_____

_____

_____

_____

_____

➤ How can you become more mindful of the things of God?

_____

_____

_____

_____

_____

➤ What profitable things can you gain during your life on earth which will actually go with you when you go to heaven?

_____

_____

_____

_____

_____

➤ In what ways can God's Word feed a person's soul?

_____

_____

_____

_____

_____

➢ What signs do you see which help you believe God is real?

_____

_____

_____

_____

_____

➢ What signs do you see which indicate Jesus really is God's Son?

_____

_____

_____

_____

_____

➢ Why do you have to watch out for the traditions and teachings of self-righteous church leaders?

_____

_____

_____

_____

_____

ACTION ITEM:

➢ Decide on one activity you can begin to increase your knowledge of God during your lifetime. What will you do to learn more about God?

_____

_____

_____

Implement your plan!

WHAT'S NEXT?

In the next chapter, take note of who the disciples see on the mountain with Jesus. It's important to note these people are alive, walking around, and visible to the disciples. Also, you'll witness the effect of belief and doubt on miracles again in the next chapter.

9 LORD OF THE LIVING

He said to them, *"Most certainly I tell you, there are some standing here who will in no way taste death until they see God's Kingdom come with power."*

After six days Jesus took with him Peter, James, and John, and brought them up onto a high mountain privately by themselves, and he was changed into another form in front of them. His clothing became glistening, exceedingly white, like snow, such as no launderer on earth can whiten them. Elijah and Moses appeared to them, and they were talking with Jesus.

Peter answered Jesus, "Rabbi, it is good for us to be here. Let's make three tents: one for you, one for Moses, and one for Elijah." For he didn't know what to say, for they were very afraid.

A cloud came, overshadowing them, and a voice came out of the cloud, *"This is my beloved Son. Listen to him."*

Suddenly looking around, they saw no one with them anymore, except Jesus only.

As they were coming down from the mountain, he commanded them that they should tell no one what things they had seen, until after the Son of Man had risen from the dead. They kept this saying to themselves, questioning what the "rising from the dead" meant.

They asked him, saying, "Why do the scribes say that Elijah must come first?"

He said to them, *"Elijah indeed comes first, and restores all things. How is it written about the Son of Man, that he should suffer many things and be despised? But I tell you that Elijah has come, and they have also done to him whatever they wanted to, even as it is written about him."*

Coming to the disciples, he saw a great multitude around them, and scribes questioning them. Immediately the entire multitude, when they saw him, were greatly amazed, and running to him, greeted him. He asked the scribes, *"What are you asking them?"*

One of the multitude answered, "Teacher, I brought to you my son, who has a mute spirit; and wherever it seizes him, it throws him down, and he foams at the mouth, and grinds his teeth, and wastes away. I asked your disciples to cast it out, and they weren't able."

He answered him, *"Unbelieving generation, how long shall I be with you? How long shall I bear with you?*

Bring him to me."

They brought him to him, and when he saw him, immediately the spirit convulsed him, and he fell on the ground, wallowing and foaming at the mouth.

He asked his father, *"How long has it been since this has come to him?"*

He said, "From childhood. Often it has cast him both into the fire and into the water to destroy him. But if you can do anything, have compassion on us, and help us."

Jesus said to him, *"If you can believe, all things are possible to him who believes."*

Immediately the father of the child cried out with tears, "I believe. Help my unbelief!"

When Jesus saw that a multitude came running together, he rebuked the unclean spirit, saying to him, *"You mute and deaf spirit, I command you, come out of him, and never enter him again!"*

After crying out and convulsing him greatly, it came out of him. The boy became like one dead, so much that most of them said, "He is dead." But Jesus took him by the hand, and raised him up; and he arose.

When he had come into the house, his disciples asked him privately, "Why couldn't we cast it out?"

He said to them, *"This kind can come out by nothing, except by prayer and fasting."*

They went out from there, and passed through Galilee. He didn't want anyone to know it. For he was teaching his disciples, and said to them, *"The Son of Man is being handed over to the hands of men, and they will kill him; and when he is killed, on the third day he will rise again."*

But they didn't understand the saying, and were afraid to ask him.

He came to Capernaum, and when he was in the house he asked them, *"What were you arguing among yourselves on the way?"*

But they were silent, for they had disputed with one another on the way about who was the greatest.

He sat down, and called the twelve; and he said to them, *"If any man wants to be first, he shall be last of all, and servant of all."*

He took a little child, and set him in the middle of them. Taking him in his arms, he said to them, *"Whoever receives one such little child in my name, receives me, and whoever receives me, doesn't receive me, but him who sent me."*

John said to him, "Teacher, we saw someone who doesn't follow us casting out demons in your name; and we forbade him, because he doesn't follow us."

But Jesus said, *"Don't forbid him, for there is no one who will do a mighty work in my name, and be able quickly to speak evil of me. For whoever is not against us is on our side. For whoever will give you a cup of water to drink in my name, because you are Christ's, most certainly I tell you, he will in no way lose his reward.*

"Whoever will cause one of these little ones who believe in me to stumble, it would be better for him if he were thrown into the sea with a millstone hung around his neck.

"If your hand causes you to stumble, cut it off. It is better for you to enter into life maimed, rather than having your two hands to go into Gehenna, into the unquenchable fire, 'where their worm doesn't die, and the fire is not quenched.'

"If your foot causes you to stumble, cut it off. It is better for you to enter into life lame, rather than having your two feet to be cast into Gehenna, into the fire that will never be quenched — ' where their worm doesn't die, and the fire is not quenched.'

"If your eye causes you to stumble, cast it out. It is better for you to enter into God's Kingdom with one eye, rather than having two eyes to be cast into the Gehenna of fire, 'where their worm doesn't die, and the fire is not quenched.'

"For everyone will be salted with fire, and every sacrifice will be seasoned with salt. Salt is good, but if the salt has lost its saltiness, with what will you season it? Have salt in yourselves, and be at peace with one another."

DID YOU NOTICE?

In the previous chapter, Jesus told the disciples He would rise again three days after His death. In this chapter, the disciples see Elijah and Moses alive, talking with Jesus on the mountain. From this we know Elijah and Moses are not dead and gone forever—they are alive and friends of Jesus.

This lets us know two things: Jewish people who were faithful to God under the old covenant are saved, even if they weren't perfect. We also know there is life after death—In Luke 20:37-38, Jesus says, "*Even Moses demonstrates that the dead are raised, in the passage about the burning bush. For he calls the Lord 'the God of Abraham, the God of Isaac, and the God of Jacob.' He is not the God of the dead but of the living, for to Him all are alive.*"

➤ After reading this chapter, what are your thoughts about life after death?

_____

_____

_____

_____

_____

_____

_____

_____

WHAT DO YOU THINK?

➤ If you witnessed the transfiguration personally, how do you think it would change the commitment you have toward God and following Jesus?

_____

_____

_____

_____

_____

_____

_____

➢ What do we know about Elijah's and Moses' state of being, based on their appearance with Jesus at His Transfiguration?

_____

_____

_____

_____

_____

➢ How does it change your feelings about death to know your spirit will never die, but you will be transformed at death?

_____

_____

_____

_____

_____

➢ Why do you think some miracles only occur with prayer and fasting?

_____

_____

_____

_____

_____

➢ What are some reasons God might not answer our prayers in a way that we expect?

_____

_____

_____

_____

_____

➤ What do you think Jesus meant when He said, "*If any man wants to be first, he shall be last of all, and servant of all?*"

_____

_____

_____

_____

_____

➤ How comfortable are you being last, rather than being first?

_____

_____

_____

_____

_____

➤ How is being willing to be last a sign of your willingness to serve others?

_____

_____

_____

_____

_____

➤ How can fiery trials and salty relationships improve and refine your character?

_____

_____

_____

_____

_____

_____

➤ If all things are possible when you believe, what positive change in yourself or in your family can you ask God for in complete faith? (Ask for it in your prayers!)

_____

_____

_____

_____

_____

_____

_____

ACTION ITEM:

Begin praying sincerely, regularly, and believing the positive change you would like to see in yourself or your family is possible!

WHAT'S NEXT?

In the next chapter, take note of Jesus' teachings about leading, being first, and how to be great among men. Jesus teaches ways that are different than typical, worldly leadership.

10 THE RIGHT WAY

Jesus arose from there and came into the borders of Judea and beyond the Jordan. Multitudes came together to him again. As he usually did, he was again teaching them. Pharisees came to him testing him, and asked him, "Is it lawful for a man to divorce his wife?"

He answered, *"What did Moses command you?"*

They said, "Moses allowed a certificate of divorce to be written, and to divorce her."

But Jesus said to them, *"For your hardness of heart, he wrote you this commandment. But from the beginning of the creation, God made them male and female. For this cause a man will leave his father and mother, and will join to his wife, and the two will become one flesh, so that they are no longer two, but one flesh. What therefore God has joined together, let no man separate."*

In the house, his disciples asked him again about the same matter. He said to them, *"Whoever divorces his wife, and marries another, commits adultery against her. If a woman herself divorces her husband, and marries another, she commits adultery."*

They were bringing to him little children, that he should touch them, but the disciples rebuked those who were bringing them. But when Jesus saw it, he was moved with indignation, and said to them, *"Allow the little children to come to me! Don't forbid them, for God's Kingdom belongs to such as these. Most certainly I tell you, whoever will not receive God's Kingdom like a little child, he will in no way enter into it."* He took them in his arms, and blessed them, laying his hands on them.

As he was going out into the way, one ran to him, knelt before him, and asked him, "Good Teacher, what shall I do that I may inherit eternal life?"

Jesus said to him, *"Why do you call me good? No one is good except one— God. You know the commandments: 'Do not murder,' 'Do not commit adultery,' 'Do not steal,' 'Do not give false testimony,' 'Do not defraud,' 'Honor your father and mother.'"*

He said to him, "Teacher, I have observed all these things from my youth." Jesus looking at him loved him, and said to him, *"One thing you lack. Go, sell* whatever you have, and give to the poor, and you will have treasure in heaven; and come, follow me, taking up the cross."

But his face fell at that saying, and he went away sorrowful, for he was one who had great possessions. Jesus looked around, and said to his disciples, *"How difficult it is for those who have riches to enter into God's Kingdom!"*

The disciples were amazed at his words. But Jesus answered again, *"Children, how hard it is for those who trust in riches to enter into God's Kingdom! It is easier for a camel to go through a needle's eye than for a rich man to enter into God's Kingdom."*

They were exceedingly astonished, saying to him, "Then who can be saved?"

Jesus, looking at them, said, *"With men it is impossible, but not with God, for all things are possible with God."*

Peter began to tell him, "Behold, we have left all, and have followed you."

Jesus said, *"Most certainly I tell you, there is no one who has left house, or brothers, or sisters, or father, or mother, or wife, or children, or land, for my sake, and for the sake of the Good News, but he will receive one hundred times more now in this time: houses, brothers, sisters, mothers, children, and land, with persecutions; and in the age to come eternal life. But many who are first will be last; and the last first."*

They were on the way, going up to Jerusalem; and Jesus was going in front of them, and they were amazed; and those who followed were afraid. He again took the twelve, and began to tell them the things that were going to happen to him. *"Behold, we are going up to Jerusalem. The Son of Man will be delivered to the chief priests and the scribes. They will condemn him to death, and will deliver him to the Gentiles. They will mock him, spit on him, scourge him, and kill him. On the third day he will rise again."*

James and John, the sons of Zebedee, came near to him, saying, "Teacher, we want you to do for us whatever we will ask."

He said to them, *"What do you want me to do for you?"*

They said to him, "Grant to us that we may sit, one at your right hand, and one at your left hand, in your glory."

But Jesus said to them, *"You don't know what you are asking. Are you able to drink the cup that I drink, and to be baptized with the baptism that I am baptized with?"*

They said to him, "We are able."

Jesus said to them, *"You shall indeed drink the cup that I drink, and you shall be baptized with the baptism that I am baptized with; but to sit at my right hand and at my left hand is not mine to give, but for whom it has been prepared."*

When the ten heard it, they began to be indignant toward James and John.

Jesus summoned them, and said to them, *"You know that they who are recognized as rulers over the nations lord it over them, and their great ones exercise authority over them. But it shall not be so among you, but whoever wants to become great among you shall be your servant. Whoever of you wants to become first among you, shall be bondservant of all. For the Son of Man also came not to be served, but to serve, and to give his life as a ransom for many."*

They came to Jericho. As he went out from Jericho, with his disciples and a great multitude, the son of Timaeus, Bartimaeus, a blind beggar, was sitting by the road. When he heard that it was Jesus the Nazarene, he began to cry out, and say, "Jesus, you son of David, have mercy on me!" Many rebuked him, that he should be quiet, but he cried out much more, "You son of David, have mercy on me!"

Jesus stood still, and said, *"Call him."*

They called the blind man, saying to him, "Cheer up! Get up. He is calling you!"

He, casting away his cloak, sprang up, and came to Jesus.

Jesus asked him, *"What do you want me to do for you?"*

The blind man said to him, "Rabboni, that I may see again."

Jesus said to him, *"Go your way. Your faith has made you well."* Immediately he received his sight, and followed Jesus on the way.

DID YOU NOTICE?

This chapter gave details about divorce, inheriting eternal life, and Jesus's kind of leadership. Did you notice the differences between how people typically behave in today's society versus what Jesus taught about divorce, receiving God's Kingdom like a child, inheriting eternal life, and leading by serving? Jesus taught us the right way to do things, and the right way hasn't changed. What do you think the consequences will be for people who no longer behave or think rightly according to Jesus' teachings?

_____

_____

_____

_____

_____

_____

_____

_____

WHAT DO YOU THINK?

➤ In what ways is it impossible for married people to completely separate their lives from each other simply by getting a divorce? What remains forever connected?

_____

_____

_____

_____

_____

➤ What do you think it means to receive God's Kingdom like a child?

_____

_____

_____

_____

_____

_____

➢ Why do you think it is difficult for rich people to enter into God's Kingdom?

_____

_____

_____

_____

_____

_____

➢ Why do you think those who followed Jesus during His life on earth were frightened by what Jesus said and did? In what ways might you be afraid if you saw and heard Jesus first hand?

_____

_____

_____

_____

_____

_____

➢ How is Jesus' leadership model different from a typical leader's behavior today?

_____

_____

_____

_____

_____

➢ With what you know about Jesus and His teachings now, what relational or leadership skills would you like for God to grow in you? Pray for that growth!

_____

_____

_____

_____

_____

_____

➤ Which of the Commandments that Jesus listed do you have the most difficulty obeying?

_____

_____

_____

_____

_____

_____

➤ What sorts of things can you do to improve your obedience to God's Commandments?

_____

_____

_____

_____

_____

_____

➤ Those who are first on Earth will be last in heaven, and those who are last on Earth will be first in heaven. How does this fact change the way you want to relate to other people while on Earth?

_____

_____

_____

_____

_____

➤ If you rated yourself on a scale of being a servant versus being served, where would you fall on a scale?

I Serve Others								I'm Served by Others
	1	2	3	4	5	6	7	

➢ Jesus said whoever desires to be great shall be a servant or slave of all. On the scale above, the closer you are to a 7, the more likely you are to end up being a slave of all. What are some things you can do to serve others now?

_____

_____

_____

_____

_____

_____

ACTION ITEM:

➢ Think of someone or somewhere you can serve. Make a plan to serve them.

_____

_____

_____

_____

_____

WHAT'S NEXT?

In the next chapter, look for Jesus' humble authority versus the demanding authority of the chief priests, scribes, and elders. Ask yourself, "From where does Jesus' authority come?"

11 AUTHORITY AND ASKING

When they came near to Jerusalem, to Bethsphage and Bethany, at the Mount of Olives, he sent two of his disciples, and said to them, *"Go your way into the village that is opposite you. Immediately as you enter into it, you will find a young donkey tied, on which no one has sat. Untie him, and bring him. If anyone asks you, 'Why are you doing this?' say, 'The Lord needs him;' and immediately he will send him back here."*

They went away, and found a young donkey tied at the door outside in the open street, and they untied him.

Some of those who stood there asked them, "What are you doing, untying the young donkey?" They said to them just as Jesus had said, and they let them go.

They brought the young donkey to Jesus, and threw their garments on it, and Jesus sat on it. Many spread their garments on the way, and others were cutting down branches from the trees, and spreading them on the road. Those who went in front, and those who followed, cried out, "Hosanna! Blessed is he who comes in the name of the Lord! Blessed is the kingdom of our father David that is coming in the name of the Lord! Hosanna in the highest!"

Jesus entered into the temple in Jerusalem. When he had looked around at everything, it being now evening, he went out to Bethany with the twelve.

The next day, when they had come out from Bethany, he was hungry. Seeing a fig tree afar off having leaves, he came to see if perhaps he might find anything on it.

When he came to it, he found nothing but leaves, for it was not the season for figs. Jesus told it, *"May no one ever eat fruit from you again!"* and his disciples heard it.

They came to Jerusalem, and Jesus entered into the temple, and began to throw out those who sold and those who bought in the temple, and overthrew the money changers' tables, and the seats of those who sold the doves. He would not allow anyone to carry a container through the temple. He taught, saying to them, *"Isn't it written, 'My house will be called a house of prayer for all the nations?' But you have made it a den of robbers!"*

The chief priests and the scribes heard it, and sought how they might destroy him. For they feared him, because all the multitude was astonished at his teaching.

When evening came, he went out of the city. As they passed by in the morning, they saw the fig tree withered away from the roots. Peter, remembering, said to him, "Rabbi, look! The fig tree which you cursed has withered away."

Jesus answered them, *"Have faith in God. For most certainly I tell you, whoever may tell this mountain, 'Be taken up and cast into the sea,' and doesn't doubt in his heart, but believes that what he says is happening; he shall have whatever he says. Therefore I tell you, all things whatever you pray and ask for, believe that you have received them, and you shall have them.*

"Whenever you stand praying, forgive, if you have anything against anyone; so that your Father, who is in heaven, may also forgive you your transgressions. But if you do not forgive, neither will your Father in heaven forgive your transgressions."

They came again to Jerusalem, and as he was walking in the temple, the chief priests, the scribes, and the elders came to him, and they began saying to him, "By what authority do you do these things? Or who gave you this authority to do these things?"

Jesus said to them, *"I will ask you one question. Answer me, and I will tell you by what authority I do these things. The baptism of John—was it from*

_____

_____

_____

_____

_____

_____

_____

_____

_____

heaven, or from men? Answer me."

They reasoned with themselves, saying, "If we should say, 'From heaven;' he will say, 'Why then did you not believe him?' If we should say, 'From men' they feared the people, for all held John to really be a prophet. They answered Jesus, "We don't know."

Jesus said to them, *"Neither do I tell you by what authority I do these things."*

DID YOU NOTICE?

This is one chapter in the Bible where Jesus is clearly upset by a figless tree and selling in the temple. Since Jesus was fully human, but also righteous in every way, it's important to reflect on why Jesus was not happy in these circumstances.

➢ Ask yourself, what is a fig tree's main purpose? The figless tree should have had figs, but it didn't. How might this beautiful, but figless tree relate to people who like to pretend they're godly, but aren't?

_____

_____

_____

_____

_____

➢ In the temple, we need to consider the purpose of God's house. The main purpose of the temple is to have a place for prayer, worship, thanksgiving, and learning in an environment wholly dedicated to God. Why is it important for us to keep God's temple Holy?

_____

_____

_____

_____

_____

_____

WHAT DO YOU THINK?

➢ Just as Jesus told His disciples what would happen before it occurred, God also tells us what will happen in the future. How can reading your Bible prepare you for the future?

_____

_____

_____

_____

_____

➢ The Fig tree represents people who act like they are faithful. Why do you think it's so upsetting to Jesus when people lack true faith and only outwardly act religious?

_____

_____

_____

_____

➢ What do you see happening in some modern churches, outside of offerings, which makes them look like dens for thieves, rather than a house of prayer for all people?

_____

_____

_____

_____

➢ In Jesus' paragraph about prayer and believing, what is the one warning Jesus gives regarding forgiveness? How does this relate to the golden rule: Do unto others as you would have them do unto you?

_____

_____

_____

_____

_____

➢ What motivations do you think the priests, scribes, and elders of the church had when they set their minds on getting rid of Jesus? Why were they so determined to stop Jesus?

_____

_____

_____

_____

_____

➢ Why do you think Jesus refused to answer the questions of the priests, scribes, and elders?

_____

_____

_____

_____

_____

➢ Why do you think it's important for you to forgive others if you want God to forgive your sins?

_____

_____

_____

_____

➢ How might your life be more effective if you live under God's Authority rather than under your own power?

_____

_____

_____

_____

_____

➤ How can you learn more about God's instructions for living life righteously?

_____

_____

_____

_____

_____

_____

ACTION ITEM:

God's word is authoritative. To fully understand it, a person must read all of the Bible. Consider finding a Bible reading plan to read the whole Bible, and establish the habit of reading your Bible daily. You can find a variety of reading plans at: https://www.biblegateway.com/reading-plans/. See if you can find one you want to use.

WHAT'S NEXT?

In the next chapter, look for the Pharisees' and scribes' continued questioning of Jesus. Think about their possible motives, as they continue trying to trap Jesus. If they think Jesus is wise, honest, and teaches the ways of God, why do they hope to trap Jesus with their questioning? What do you think they hope to accomplish?

12 TOP COMMAND

He began to speak to them in parables. *"A man planted a vineyard, put a hedge around it, dug a pit for the wine press, built a tower, rented it out to a farmer, and went into another country. When it was time, he sent a servant to the farmer to get from the farmer his share of the fruit of the vineyard. They took him, beat him, and sent him away empty. Again, he sent another servant to them; and they threw stones at him, wounded him in the head, and sent him away shamefully treated. Again he sent another; and they killed him; and many others, beating some, and killing some. Therefore still having one, his beloved son, he sent him last to them, saying, 'They will respect my son.' But those farmers said among themselves, 'This is the heir. Come, let's kill him, and the inheritance will be ours.' They took him,* _killed him, and cast him out of the vineyard. What therefore will the lord of the vineyard do? He will come and destroy the farmers, and will give the vineyard to others._

"Haven't you even read this Scripture: 'The stone which the builders rejected was made the head of the corner. This was from the Lord. It is marvelous in our eyes'?"

They tried to seize him, but they feared the multitude; for they perceived that he spoke the parable against them. They left him, and went away. They sent some of the Pharisees and the Herodians to him, that they might trap him with words. When they had come, they asked him, "Teacher, we know that you are honest, and don't defer to anyone; for you aren't partial to anyone, but truly teach the way of God. Is it lawful to pay taxes to Caesar, or not? Shall we give, or shall we not give?"

But he, knowing their hypocrisy, said to them, _"Why do you test me? Bring me a denarius, that I may see it."_

They brought it.

He said to them, _"Whose is this image and inscription?"_ They said to him, "Caesar's."

Jesus answered them, _"Render to Caesar the things that are Caesar's, and to God the things that are God's."_

They marveled greatly at him.

Some Sadducees, who say that there is no resurrection, came to him. They asked him, saying, "Teacher, Moses wrote to us, 'If a man's brother dies, and leaves a wife behind him, and leaves no children, that his brother should take his wife, and raise up offspring for his brother.' There were seven brothers. The first took a wife, and dying left no offspring. The second took her, and died, leaving no children behind him. The third likewise; and the seven took her and left no children. Last of all the woman also died. In the resurrection, when they rise, whose wife will she be of them? For the seven had her as a wife."

Jesus answered them, *"Isn't this because you are mistaken, not knowing the Scriptures, nor the power of God? For when they will rise from the dead, they neither marry, nor are given in marriage, but are like angels in heaven. But about the dead, that they are raised; haven't you read in the book of Moses, about the Bush, how God spoke to him, saying, 'I am the God of Abraham, the God of Isaac, and the God of Jacob'? He is not the God of the dead, but of the living. You are therefore badly mistaken."*

One of the scribes came, and heard them questioning together, and knowing that he had answered them well, asked him, "Which commandment is the greatest of all?"

Jesus answered, *"The greatest is, 'Hear, Israel, the Lord our God, the Lord is one: you shall love the Lord your God with all your heart, and with all your soul, and with all your mind, and with all your strength.' This is the first commandment. The second is like this, 'You shall love your neighbor as* _yourself.' There is no other commandment greater than these."_

The scribe said to him, "Truly, teacher, you have said well that he is one, and there is none other but he, and to love him with all the heart, and with all the understanding, with all the soul, and with all the strength, and to love his neighbor as himself, is more important than all whole burnt offerings and sacrifices." When Jesus saw that he answered wisely, he said to him, _"You are not far from God's Kingdom."_

No one dared ask him any question after that. Jesus responded, as he taught in the temple, _"How is it that the scribes say that the Christ is the son of David? For David himself said in the Holy Spirit, 'The Lord said to my Lord, "Sit at my right hand, until I make your enemies the footstool of your feet."' Therefore David himself calls him Lord, so how can he be his son?"_

The common people heard him gladly. In his teaching he said to them, _"Beware of the scribes, who like to walk in long robes, and to get greetings in the marketplaces, and the best seats in the synagogues, and the best places at feasts: those who devour widows' houses, and for a pretense make long prayers. These will receive greater condemnation."_

Jesus sat down opposite the treasury, and saw how the multitude cast money into the treasury. Many who were rich cast in much. A poor widow came, and she cast in two small brass coins, which equal a quadrans coin. He called his disciples to himself, and said to them, *"Most certainly I tell you, this poor widow gave more than all those who are giving into the treasury, for they all gave out of their abundance, but she, out of her poverty, gave all that she had to live on."*

_____
_____
_____
_____
_____
_____

DID YOU NOTICE?

Jesus answered the Pharisees and Sadducees wisely when they questioned and tried to trap Him. The Pharisees, Sadducees, as well as the Jewish people and Muslims of today, believe in the Old Testament. However, they don't believe Jesus fulfills prophecies of the Messiah as described in the scriptures, even though the prophesies in the books of Daniel 9:24-27, Ezekiel 37:26-27, Isaiah 53, Jeremiah 31:15, Haggai 2:6-9, and others don't (and can't) point to anyone else at this point in history.

The scriptures say, "They marveled greatly at him." If the church officials marveled greatly about Jesus, why didn't they believe Jesus is the son of God? HINT: In the first sentence of Jesus' answer about the seven brothers who had one woman as their wife, Jesus tells why they don't believe Him.

_____
_____
_____
_____
_____

WHAT DO YOU THINK?

➤ What things in life belong to God? How can you use those things to benefit God?

_____
_____
_____
_____
_____
_____

➢ What do you think it will be like to rise from the dead and be like an angel in heaven?

_____

_____

_____

_____

_____

➢ What does it mean when Jesus says, *"He is not the God of the dead, but of the living?"* (Think back to the transfiguration in chapter 9.)

_____

_____

_____

_____

_____

➢ Why do you think it's difficult for many people to believe Jesus is God's Messenger and Son?

_____

_____

_____

_____

_____

_____

➢ Jesus didn't care what anyone else thought, nor what their status was in society. How does it benefit us to disregard who anyone is or what they think of us?

_____

_____

_____

_____

_____

➢ How can you increase your scriptural knowledge and the power of God within?

_____

_____

_____

_____

_____

➢ If God is the god of the living, who do you believe is now living with God besides Abraham, Isaac, Jacob, Moses, and Elijah?

_____

_____

_____

_____

_____

_____

➢ How can you better live out the most important commandment to love God with all of your heart, soul, mind and strength?

_____

_____

_____

_____

_____

➢ How can you love yourself better, so that you can love your neighbor as yourself?

_____

_____

_____

_____

_____

> What kinds of things can you do to show love to your neighbor?

_____

_____

_____

_____

_____

ACTION ITEM:

> Who do you know that needs love and support in their life? Think of some ways to encourage that person, and do something to encourage them.

_____

_____

_____

_____

_____

_____

WHAT'S NEXT?

In the next chapter, look for the signs of the end times. Take note of how society and the earth show signs of things to come. Jesus gives us clear information about what the end times will be like.

13 END TIMES EXPLAINED

As he went out of the temple, one of his disciples said to him, "Teacher, see what kind of stones and what kind of buildings!"

Jesus said to him, *"Do you see these great buildings? There will not be left here one stone on another, which will not be thrown down."*

As he sat on the Mount of Olives opposite the temple, Peter, James, John, and Andrew asked him privately, "Tell us, when will these things be? What is the sign that these things are all about to be fulfilled?"

Jesus, answering, began to tell them, *"Be careful that no one leads you astray. For many will come in my name, saying, 'I am he!' and will lead many astray. "When you hear of wars and rumors of wars, don't be troubled. For those must happen, but the end is not* yet. For nation will rise against nation, and kingdom against kingdom. There will be earthquakes in various places. There will be famines and troubles. These things are the beginning of birth pains. But watch yourselves, for they will deliver you up to councils. You will be beaten in synagogues. You will stand before rulers and kings for my sake, for a testimony to them. The Good News must first be preached to all the nations. When they lead you away and deliver you up, don't be anxious beforehand, or premeditate what you will say, but say whatever will be given you in that hour. For it is not you who speak, but the Holy Spirit.

"Brother will deliver up brother to death, and the father his child. Children will rise up against parents, and cause them to be put to death. You will be hated by all men for my name's sake, but he who endures to the end will be saved. But when you see the abomination of desolation, spoken of by Daniel the prophet, standing where it ought not" (let the reader understand), "then let those who are in Judea flee to the mountains, and let him who is on the housetop not go down, nor enter in, to take anything out of his house. Let him who is in the field not return back to take his cloak.

"But woe to those who are with child and to those who nurse babies in those days! Pray that your flight won't be in the winter. For in those days there will be oppression, such as there has not been the like from the beginning of the creation which God created until now, and never will be. Unless the Lord had shortened the days, no flesh would have been saved; but for the sake of the chosen ones, whom he picked out, he shortened the days. Then if anyone tells you, 'Look, here is the Christ!' or, 'Look, there!' don't believe it. For there will arise false christs and false prophets, and will show signs and wonders, that they may lead astray, if possible, even the chosen ones. But you watch.

"Behold, I have told you all things beforehand. But in those days, after that oppression, the sun will be darkened, the moon will not give its light, the stars will be falling from the sky, and the powers that are in the heavens will be shaken. Then they will see the Son of Man coming in clouds with great power and glory. Then he will send out his angels, and will gather together his chosen ones from the four winds, from the ends of the earth to the ends of the sky.

"Now from the fig tree, learn this parable. When the branch has now become tender, and produces its leaves, you know that the summer is near; even so you also, when you see these things coming to pass, know that it is near, at the doors. Most certainly I say to you, this generation will not pass away until all these things happen. Heaven and earth will pass away, but my words will

_____

_____

_____

_____

_____

_____

_____

_____

_____

_____

_____

_____

_____

_____

_____

not pass away. But of that day or that hour no one knows, not even the angels in heaven, nor the Son, but only the Father. Watch, keep alert, and pray; for you don't know when the time is.

"It is like a man, traveling to another country, having left his house, and given authority to his servants, and to each one his work, and also commanded the doorkeeper to keep watch. Watch therefore, for you don't know when the lord of the house is coming, whether at evening, or at midnight, or when the rooster crows, or in the morning; lest coming suddenly he might find you sleeping. What I tell you, I tell all: Watch."

DID YOU NOTICE?

Did you notice some end time events are already taking place? According to Jesus, the end of this era will occur when his Good News about grace and salvation has been preached to all nations. Once everyone has heard the Good News, and made their decision about whether to be saved by Jesus (or not), He will return to gather His followers.

With the description given of the end times events, it's difficult to imagine remaining calm and peaceful. However, according to scriptures (Philippians 4:6-7), God gives us a peace that surpasses all understanding. I don't know about you, but I think I will need a large measure of God's peace when the end times are at their fullest level of persecution against Christians!

WHAT DO YOU THINK?

➤ What scares you or concerns you most about the end times?

_____

_____

_____

_____

_____

➢ Jesus said many will be led astray in the end times. What steps can you take to make sure you are not led astray by powerful or charismatic leaders?

_____

_____

_____

_____

_____

➢ Who or what are some of the deceivers which are present in the world today?

_____

_____

_____

_____

_____

_____

➢ What kinds of things could lead you away from a close relationship with God?

_____

_____

_____

_____

_____

_____

➢ Which of the signs of the end times do you see in the world already?

_____

_____

_____

_____

_____

_____

➤ In your opinion, how near are the end times? What makes you believe that?

_____
_____
_____
_____
_____

➤ Jesus said, *"The Good News must first be preached to all the nations,"* before the end actually comes. What places or groups in the world's population do you think still need to hear the Good News?

_____
_____
_____
_____
_____

➤ What evidence do you see the gospel is being preached to nearly all Nations today?

_____
_____
_____
_____
_____

➤ Think about what the Holy Spirit may want to tell others through you. What important message would you like to share with the world?

_____
_____
_____
_____
_____
_____

➤ Analyze the strength of your faith in Jesus. What weakens your faith and what makes it stronger?

_____

_____

_____

_____

_____

_____

ACTION ITEM:

Watch for signs of the end times and pray for protection from deception.

WHAT'S NEXT?

In the next chapter, Jesus establishes the practice we know as communion. Pay attention to the bread and wine as symbols of Jesus' sacrifice for you, me, and the rest of the world.

14 FIRST COMMUNION

It was now two days before the feast of the Passover and the unleavened bread, and the chief priests and the scribes sought how they might seize him by deception, and kill him. For they said, "Not during the feast, because there might be a riot among the people."

While he was at Bethany, in the house of Simon the leper, as he sat at the table, a woman came having an alabaster jar of ointment of pure nard—very costly. She broke the jar, and poured it over his head. But there were some who were indignant among themselves, saying, "Why has this ointment been wasted? For this might have been sold for more than three hundred denarii, and given to the poor." So they grumbled against her.

But Jesus said, *"Leave her alone. Why do you trouble her? She has done a good work for me. For you always have* _the poor with you, and whenever you want to, you can do them good; but you will not always have me. She has done what she could. She has anointed my body beforehand for the burying. Most certainly I tell you, wherever this Good News may be preached throughout the whole world, that which this woman has done will also be spoken of for a memorial of her."_

Judas Iscariot, who was one of the twelve, went away to the chief priests, that he might deliver him to them. They, when they heard it, were glad, and promised to give him money. He sought how he might conveniently deliver him. On the first day of unleavened bread, when they sacrificed the Passover, his disciples asked him, "Where do you want us to go and prepare that you may eat the Passover?"

He sent two of his disciples, and said to them, _"Go into the city, and there you will meet a man carrying a pitcher of water. Follow him, and wherever he enters in, tell the master of the house, 'The Teacher says, "Where is the guest room, where I may eat the Passover with my disciples?"' He will himself show you a large upper room furnished and ready. Get ready for us there."_

His disciples went out, and came into the city, and found things as he had said to them, and they prepared the Passover.

When it was evening he came with the twelve. As they sat and were eating, Jesus said, _"Most certainly I tell you, one of_ you will betray me—he who eats with me."

They began to be sorrowful, and to ask him one by one, "Surely not I?" And another said, "Surely not I?"

He answered them, *"It is one of the twelve, he who dips with me in the dish. For the Son of Man goes, even as it is written about him, but woe to that man by whom the Son of Man is betrayed! It would be better for that man if he had not been born."*

As they were eating, Jesus took bread, and when he had blessed, he broke it, and gave to them, and said, *"Take, eat. This is my body."*

He took the cup, and when he had given thanks, he gave to them. They all drank of it. He said to them, *"This is my blood of the new covenant, which is poured out for many. Most certainly I tell you, I will no more drink of the fruit of the vine, until that day when I drink it anew in God's Kingdom."*

When they had sung a hymn, they went out to the Mount of Olives.

Jesus said to them, *"All of you will be made to stumble because of me tonight, for it is written, 'I will strike the shepherd, and the sheep will be scattered.' However, after I am raised up, I will go before you into Galilee."*

But Peter said to him, "Although all will be offended, yet I will not."

Jesus said to him, *"Most certainly I tell you, that you today, even this night, before the rooster crows twice, you will deny me three times."*

But he spoke all the more, "If I must die with you, I will not deny you." They all said the same thing.

They came to a place which was named Gethsemane. He said to his disciples, *"Sit here, while I pray."* He took with him Peter, James, and John, and began to be greatly troubled and distressed. He said to them, *"My soul is exceedingly sorrowful, even to death. Stay here, and watch."*

He went forward a little, and fell on the ground, and prayed that, if it were possible, the hour might pass away from him. He said, *"Abba, Father, all things are possible to you. Please remove this cup from me. However, not what I desire, but what you desire."*

He came and found them sleeping, and said to Peter, *"Simon, are you sleeping? Couldn't you watch one hour? Watch and pray, that you may not enter into temptation. The spirit indeed is willing, but the flesh is weak."*

Again he went away, and prayed, saying the same words. Again he returned, and found them sleeping, for their eyes were very heavy, and they didn't know what to answer him. He came the third time, and said to them, *"Sleep on now, and take your rest. It is enough. The hour has come. Behold, the Son of Man is betrayed into the hands of sinners. Arise! Let's get going. Behold: he who betrays me is at hand."*

Immediately, while he was still

speaking, Judas, one of the twelve, came —and with him a multitude with swords and clubs, from the chief priests, the scribes, and the elders. Now he who betrayed him had given them a sign, saying, "Whomever I will kiss, that is he. Seize him, and lead him away safely." When he had come, immediately he came to him, and said, "Rabbi! Rabbi!" and kissed him. They laid their hands on him, and seized him. But a certain one of those who stood by drew his sword, and struck the servant of the high priest, and cut off his ear.

Jesus answered them, *"Have you come out, as against a robber, with swords and clubs to seize me? I was daily with you in the temple But this is so that the Scriptures might be fulfilled."*

They all left him, and fled. A certain young man followed him, having a linen cloth thrown around himself over his naked body. The young men grabbed him, but he left the linen cloth, and fled from them naked. They led Jesus away to the high priest. All the chief priests, the elders, and the scribes came together with him.

Peter had followed him from a distance, until he came into the court of the high priest. He was sitting with the officers, and warming himself in the light of the fire. Now the chief priests and the whole council sought witnesses against Jesus to put him to death, and found none. For many gave false testimony against him, and their testimony didn't agree with each other.

Some stood up, and gave false testimony against him, saying, "We heard him say, 'I will destroy this temple that is made with hands, and in three days I will build another made without hands.'" Even so, their testimony didn't agree.

The high priest stood up in the middle, and asked Jesus, "Have you no answer? What is it which these testify against you?" But he stayed quiet, and answered nothing. Again the high priest asked him, "Are you the Christ, the Son of the Blessed?"

Jesus said, *"I am. You will see the Son of Man sitting at the right hand of Power, and coming with the clouds of the sky."*

The high priest tore his clothes, and said, "What further need have we of witnesses? You have heard the blasphemy! What do you think?" They all condemned him to be worthy of death. Some began to spit on him, and to cover his face, and to beat him with fists, and to tell him, "Prophesy!" The officers struck him with the palms of their hands.

As Peter was in the courtyard below, one of the maids of the high priest came, and seeing Peter warming himself, she looked at him, and said, "You were also with the Nazarene, Jesus!"

But he denied it, saying, "I neither know, nor understand what you are saying." He went out on the porch, and the rooster crowed.

The maid saw him, and began again to tell those who stood by, "This is one of them." But he again denied it. After a little while again those who stood by said to Peter, "You truly are one of them, for you are a Galilean, and your speech shows it." But he began to curse, and to swear, "I don't know this man of whom you speak!"

The rooster crowed the second time. Peter remembered the word, how that Jesus said to him, *"Before the rooster crows twice, you will deny me three times."* When he thought about that, he wept.

DID YOU NOTICE?

In this chapter, Jesus explained the bread is a symbol of His body and the wine symbolizes His blood. These symbolic sacrifices mean we no longer kill and sacrifice animals to atone for our sins, because Jesus died for our sins. Did you understand this significance of this first communion with bread and wine?

We eat bread and drink wine as we remember Jesus as the ultimate atoning sacrifice for our sins. Jesus calls us to take communion as often as we remember our sins and His saving grace through the sacrifice of His life.

WHAT DO YOU THINK?

➢ In order to show your love for Jesus, what kinds of good works or activities could you do which would be of service to Jesus?

➢ Many people think of themselves as godly people, like the priests—yet they were seeking to kill Jesus. Do you think they will get into Heaven? Why or why not?

➤ Jesus knew all things are possible through God, and He prayed to have His upcoming crucifixion removed. It wasn't. Why do you think God didn't answer Jesus' prayer by rescuing Him?

_____

_____

_____

_____

_____

➤ Jesus could have called down the power of God to save Himself. Why didn't Jesus fight back against His accusers or stop Judas from betraying Him?

_____

_____

_____

_____

_____

➤ What does Jesus' example teach you about fighting back when you are offended?

_____

_____

_____

_____

_____

➤ Why did all of Jesus's disciples desert Jesus when He was taken into custody? If you were a disciple, what do you think you would have done?

_____

_____

_____

_____

_____

➤ If people truly believe Jesus was resurrected to life after he died, what affect do you think it will have on their desire to know and follow Jesus?

_____

_____

_____

_____

_____

_____

➤ Why should you remain watchful against sin and pray not to enter into temptation?

_____

_____

_____

_____

_____

_____

➤ Why do you think church leaders didn't believe Jesus when He said, "*I am the Christ?*"

_____

_____

_____

_____

_____

_____

ACTION ITEM:

If you believe Jesus is God's Son, pray to be true to Jesus and all He teaches, and not to enter into temptation.

WHAT'S NEXT?

In the next chapter, notice how Jesus responds to the authorities who are condemning Him, and how the authorities give in to the chants of the blood-thirsty crowd. Consider what role you would have played if you were there during Jesus' trial and crucifixion. Consider, what would you have done if you were in authority. What would you do if you were in the crowd?

15 CRUCIFIED, DEAD, AND BURIED

Immediately in the morning the chief priests, with the elders and scribes, and the whole council, held a consultation, bound Jesus, carried him away, and delivered him up to Pilate. Pilate asked him, "Are you the King of the Jews?"

He answered, *"So you say."*

The chief priests accused him of many things. Pilate again asked him, "Have you no answer? See how many things they testify against you!"

But Jesus made no further answer, so that Pilate marveled.

Now at the feast he used to release to them one prisoner, whom they asked of him. There was one called Barabbas, bound with his fellow insurgents, men who in the insurrection had committed murder.

The multitude, crying aloud, began to ask him to do as he always did for them. Pilate answered them, saying, "Do you want me to release to you the King of the Jews?" For he perceived that for envy the chief priests had delivered him up. But the chief priests stirred up the multitude, that he should release Barabbas to them instead. Pilate again asked them, "What then should I do to him whom you call the King of the Jews?"

They cried out again, "Crucify him!"

Pilate said to them, "Why, what evil has he done?" But they cried out exceedingly, "Crucify him!"

Pilate, wishing to please the multitude, released Barabbas to them, and handed over Jesus, when he had flogged him, to be crucified. The soldiers led him away within the court, which is the Praetorium; and they called together the whole cohort. They clothed him with purple, and weaving a crown of thorns, they put it on him. They began to salute him, "Hail, King of the Jews!" They struck his head with a reed, and spat on him, and bowing their knees, did homage to him. When they had mocked him, they took the purple off him, and put his own garments on him. They led him out to crucify him. They compelled one passing by, coming from the country, Simon of Cyrene, the father of Alexander and Rufus, to go with them, that he might bear his cross. They brought him to the place called Golgotha, which is, being interpreted, "The place of a skull." They offered him wine mixed with myrrh to drink, but he didn't take it.

Crucifying him, they parted his garments among them, casting lots on them, what each should take. It was the third hour, and they crucified him. The superscription of his accusation was written over him, "THE KING OF THE JEWS." With him they crucified two robbers; one on his right hand, and one on his left. The Scripture was fulfilled, which says, "He was counted with transgressors."

Those who passed by blasphemed him, wagging their heads, and saying, "Ha! You who destroy the temple, and build it in three days, save yourself, and come down from the cross!"

Likewise, also the chief priests mocking among themselves with the scribes said, "He saved others. He can't save himself. Let the Christ, the King of Israel, now come down from the cross, that we may see and believe him." Those who were crucified with him also insulted him.

When the sixth hour had come, there was darkness over the whole land until the ninth hour. At the ninth hour Jesus cried with a loud voice, saying, *"Eloi, Eloi, lama sabachthani?"* which is, being interpreted, *"My God, my God, why have you forsaken me?"*

Some of those who stood by, when they heard it, said, "Behold, he is calling Elijah."

One ran, and filling a sponge full of vinegar, put it on a reed, and gave it to him to drink, saying, "Let him be. Let's see whether Elijah comes to take him down."

Jesus cried out with a loud voice, and gave up the spirit. The veil of the temple was torn in two from the top to the bottom. When the centurion, who stood by opposite him, saw that he cried out like this and breathed his last, he said, "Truly this man was the Son of God!"

There were also women watching from afar, among whom were both Mary Magdalene, and Mary the mother of James the less and of Joses, and Salome; who, when he was in Galilee, followed him and served him; and many other women who came up with him to Jerusalem.

When evening had now come, because it was the Preparation Day, that is, the day before the Sabbath, Joseph of Arimathaea, a prominent council member who also himself was looking for God's Kingdom, came. He boldly went in to Pilate, and asked for Jesus' body.

Pilate marveled if he were already dead; and summoning the centurion, he asked him whether he had been dead long. When he found out from the centurion, he granted the body to Joseph. He bought a linen cloth, and taking him down, wound him in the linen cloth, and laid him in a tomb which had been cut out of a rock. He rolled a stone against the door of the tomb. Mary Magdalene and Mary, the mother of Joses, saw where he was laid.

DID YOU NOTICE?

Did you notice Jesus did not try to explain Himself nor defend Himself at all? Neither did He try to save Himself from the cross. That is because He came for a purpose. Jesus knew He would be persecuted. Jesus also knew what would happen after He died. You will read about what happened after Jesus died in the next chapter.

WHAT DO YOU THINK?

➢ What kinds of desires do you think the crowd had in their hearts when they chanted for Jesus to be crucified?

_____

_____

_____

_____

_____

_____

➢ As a leader, why do you think Pilate gave in to the chants of the crowd, when he could have done what was right and let Jesus go?

_____

_____

_____

_____

_____

➢ If you were in the crowd, how do you think you would feel about the crowd's condemnation of Jesus? Why might you feel pressured to join in the chanting?

_____

_____

_____

_____

_____

_____

_____

➤ What do you think happened to the mockers and condemners of Jesus?

_____

_____

_____

_____

_____

_____

➤ For what purpose did Jesus say he had come?

_____

_____

_____

_____

_____

_____

_____

➤ Given His ministry and teachings, why do you think it is important that Jesus was crucified with Sinners?

_____

_____

_____

_____

_____

_____

➤ Since Jesus, God's beloved Son, felt forsaken by God, what do you think we need to remember in hard times when we feel like God has forgotten us?

_____

_____

_____

_____

_____

_____

> What emotions would you feel if you heard Jesus saying He is the Son of God, but then you saw Him crucified, dead and buried? What affect might it have on your faith in Jesus at that moment?

_____

_____

_____

_____

_____

_____

_____

ACTION ITEM:

Pray to have the right motives and a righteous heart when it comes to following the crowd versus going against the crowd.

WHAT'S NEXT?

Jesus came to teach us about God. He knew beforehand the religious leaders and mobs would crucify Him. Jesus came and died for the purpose of being a living sacrifice for us and our sins.

In the next chapter, notice how Jesus' resurrection, His return from death, shows He can never be killed by those who oppose Him. Consider how this single fact allows Jesus to continue influencing the world more than 2,000 years after He physically walked on Earth.

16 JESUS IS ALIVE!

When the Sabbath was past, Mary Magdalene, and Mary the mother of James, and Salome, bought spices, that they might come and anoint him. Very early on the first day of the week, they came to the tomb when the sun had risen. They were saying among themselves, "Who will roll away the stone from the door of the tomb for us?" for it was very big. Looking up, they saw that the stone was rolled back.

Entering into the tomb, they saw a young man sitting on the right side, dressed in a white robe, and they were amazed. He said to them, "Don't be amazed. You seek Jesus, the Nazarene, who has been crucified. He has risen. He is not here. Behold, the place where they laid him!

But go, tell his disciples and Peter, 'He goes before you into Galilee. There you will see him, as he said to you.'"

They went out, and fled from the tomb, for trembling and astonishment had come on them. They said nothing to anyone; for they were afraid. Now when he had risen early on the first day of the week, he appeared first to Mary Magdalene, from whom he had cast out seven demons. She went and told those who had been with him, as they mourned and wept. When they heard that he was alive, and had been seen by her, they disbelieved.

After these things he was revealed in another form to two of them, as they walked, on their way into the country. They went away and told it to the rest. They didn't believe them, either.

Afterward he was revealed to the eleven themselves as they sat at the table, and he rebuked them for their unbelief and hardness of heart, because they didn't believe those who had seen him after he had risen. He said to them, *"Go into all the world, and preach the Good News to the whole creation. He who believes and is baptized will be saved; but he who disbelieves will be condemned. These signs will accompany those who believe: in my name they will cast out demons; they will speak with new languages; they will take up serpents; and if they drink any deadly thing, it will in no way hurt them; they will lay hands on the sick, and they will recover."*

So then the Lord, after he had spoken to them, was received up into heaven, and sat down at the right hand of God. They went out, and preached everywhere, the Lord working with them, and confirming the word by the signs that followed. Amen.

DID YOU NOTICE?

Jesus' resurrection undoubtedly deepened His disciple's conviction and enthusiasm. In other words, after Jesus was raised from the dead and seen alive by His followers, there was no way anyone could convince His followers that Jesus was not the Son of God. They began spreading the news about Jesus and all He taught passionately. No one could stop Jesus' followers from that point forward, and they maintained their convictions even to the point of being put to death like Jesus.

Even though Jesus told His followers He had to die and would rise again, nobody truly expected His resurrection. When people saw Jesus dead, then saw Him alive after His resurrection, they KNEW in their hearts and souls, without a doubt—Jesus is the Son of God. After witnessing these events, no one could change their minds.

WHAT DO YOU THINK?

➢ What emotions do you think both of the Marys felt, and what do you think they thought when the man in the tomb told them Jesus is risen?

_____

_____

_____

_____

_____

_____

➢ How do you think you would feel if you heard Jesus rose from the dead after you had personally seen him crucified?

_____

_____

_____

_____

_____

_____

_____

➢ In what ways do you think seeing Jesus' resurrection changed the beliefs of His followers?

_____

_____

_____

_____

_____

➢ In chapters 8, 9, and 10, Jesus plainly tells the Apostles He will be killed and will rise again. Why do you think Jesus' apostles didn't believe Mary or the two men when they said they saw Jesus alive?

_____

_____

_____

_____

_____

➢ Based on Jesus' final instructions, what actions are required for you to be saved from sin and death?

_____

_____

_____

_____

_____

➢ God, Jesus, and the Holy Spirit are spiritual beings. Because their influence on Earth is spiritual, there is no way fleshly people can stop their influence. Why do you think some people still fight against the spread of Jesus' Good News?

_____

_____

_____

_____

_____

➤ What do you imagine the townspeople began saying and doing as Jesus appeared alive to more and more people in town?

_____

_____

_____

_____

_____

➤ If Jesus appeared before you right at this moment, what questions would you want to ask Him?

_____

_____

_____

_____

_____

➤ If you are going to go into the world to tell people about Jesus, who are the people you want to tell about Jesus first?

_____

_____

_____

_____

_____

➤ If you had lived and witnessed Jesus's life in person, how do you think your faith would be different than it is currently?

_____

_____

_____

_____

_____

_____

ACTION ITEM:

Make a definite decision about whether you will follow Jesus. If you plan to follow Him, make a plan to read a bit of your Bible every day, and begin praying to truly know Jesus.

WHAT'S NEXT?

In the next chapter, count up the number of people who saw Jesus alive after He died. It's not a small number of people!

The large number of people spreading the Good News allowed Jesus' message to spread quickly across the known world. Because Jesus is alive, victorious over death, and has paid for our sins, there is no stopping His message of Good News from spreading. His message continues to spread more than 2,000 years later.

As you read the next chapter, remember—Jesus already appeared to the two Marys, the two men on the road to Emmaus, and His Apostles in the previous chapter. Also, as you count up the number of eye-witnesses who helped spread the news about Jesus, remember there are a couple of overlaps in the eye-witness mentions between the two chapters.

BONUS: OVER 500 EYEWITNESSES

BONUS CHAPTER:

Now I declare to you, brothers, the Good News which I preached to you, which also you received, in which you also stand, by which also you are saved, if you hold firmly the word which I preached to you—unless you believed in vain. For I delivered to you first of all that which I also received: that Christ died for our sins according to the Scriptures, that he was buried, that He was raised on the third day according to the Scriptures, and that He appeared to Cephas, then to the twelve (disciples). Then He appeared to over five hundred brothers at once, most of whom remain until now, but some have also fallen asleep.

Then He appeared to James, then to all the apostles, and last of all, as to the child born at the wrong time, He appeared to me also. For I am the least of the apostles,

1 CORINTHIANS 15

_____
_____
_____
_____
_____
_____
_____
_____
_____
_____
_____
_____
_____
_____
_____
_____

who is not worthy to be called an apostle, because I persecuted the assembly of God. But by the grace of God I am what I am. His grace which was given to me was not futile, but I worked more than all of them; yet not I, but the grace of God which was with me. Whether then it is I or they, so we preach, and so you believed.

Now if Christ is preached, that He has been raised from the dead, how do some among you say that there is no resurrection of the dead? But if there is no resurrection of the dead, neither has Christ been raised. If Christ has not been raised, then our preaching is in vain, and your faith also is in vain.

Yes, we are also found false witnesses of God, because we testified about God that He raised up Christ, whom He didn't raise up, if it is so that the dead are not raised. For if the dead aren't raised, neither has Christ been raised. If Christ has not been raised, your faith is vain; you are still in your sins. Then they also who are fallen asleep in Christ have perished. If we have only hoped in Christ in this life, we are of all men most pitiable.

But now *Christ has been raised from the dead*. He became the first fruits of those who are asleep.

For since death came by man, the resurrection of the dead also came by man. For as in Adam all die, so also *in Christ all will be made alive*. But each in his own order: Christ the first fruits, then those who are Christ's, at His coming. Then the end comes, when He will deliver up the Kingdom to God, even the Father, when He will have abolished all rule and all authority and power. For He must reign until He has put all his enemies under His feet. The last enemy that will be abolished is death.

For, "He put all things in subjection under his feet."

But when He says, "All things are put in subjection", it is evident that He is excepted who subjected all things to Him. When all things have been subjected to Him, then the Son will also Himself be subjected to Him who subjected all things to Him, that God may be all in all.

Or else what will they do who are baptized for the dead? If the dead aren't raised at all, why then are they baptized for the dead? Why do we also stand in jeopardy every hour? I affirm, by the boasting in you which I have in Christ Jesus our Lord, I die daily.

If I fought with animals at Ephesus for human purposes, what does it profit me? If the dead are not raised, then "let's eat and drink, for tomorrow we die."

Don't be deceived!

"Evil companionships corrupt good morals." Wake up righteously, and don't sin, for some have no knowledge of God. I say this to your shame.

But someone will say, "How are the dead raised?" and, "With what kind of body do they come?" You foolish one, that which you yourself sow is not made alive unless it dies. That which you sow, you don't sow the body that will be, but a bare grain, maybe of wheat, or of some other kind. But God gives it a body even as it pleased Him, and to each seed a body of its own.

All flesh is not the same flesh, but there is one flesh of men, another flesh of animals, another of fish, and another of birds. There are also celestial bodies and terrestrial bodies; but the glory of the celestial differs from that of the terrestrial. There is one glory of the sun, another glory of the moon, and another glory of the stars; for one star differs from another star in glory. So also is the resurrection of the dead.

The body is sown perishable; it is raised imperishable. It is sown in dishonor; it is raised in glory. It is sown in weakness; it is raised in power. It is sown a natural body; it is raised a spiritual body. There is a natural body and there is also a spiritual body.

So also it is written, "The first man, Adam, became a living soul." The last Adam became a life-giving spirit.

However that which is spiritual isn't first, but that which is natural, then that which is spiritual. The first man is of the earth, made of dust. The second man is the Lord from heaven. As is the one made of dust, such are those who are also made of dust; and as is the heavenly, such are they also that are heavenly. As we have borne the image of those made of dust, let's also bear the image of the heavenly.

Now I say this, brothers, that flesh and blood can't inherit God's Kingdom; neither does the perishable inherit imperishable.

Behold, I tell you a mystery. We will not all sleep, but we will all be changed, in a moment, in the twinkling of an eye," at the last trumpet. For the trumpet will sound and the dead will be raised incorruptible, and we will be changed. For this perishable body must become imperishable, and this mortal must put on immortality. But when this perishable body will have become imperishable, and this mortal will have put on immortality, then what is written will happen: "Death is swallowed up in victory."

"Death, where is your sting? Hades, where is your victory?"

The sting of death is sin, and the power of sin is the law. But thanks be to God, who gives us the victory through our Lord Jesus Christ. Therefore, my beloved brothers, be steadfast, immovable, always abounding in the Lord's work, because you know that your labor is not in vain in the Lord.

DID YOU NOTICE?

Jesus appeared to more than 500 people. No doubt Jesus' appearance was quite exciting and caused the people to talk about his amazing resurrection to life. The Good News about Jesus being resurrected and alive began to spread.

In the Book of Acts 5:38-39, a Pharisee named Gamaliel told persecutors of Jesus' Apostles, "Now I tell you, withdraw from these men, and leave them alone. For if this counsel or this work is of men, it will be overthrown. But if it is of God, you will not be able to overthrow it, and you would be found even to be fighting against God!"

If Jesus was just a man, His followers would have stopped sharing Jesus' message long ago. But Jesus is evidently not just a man—His message has not been overthrown, so we can be pretty certain He is the Son of God, and He is unstoppable. Jesus' message has been unstoppable for more than 2000 years, because Jesus was speaking TRUTH. And His disciples were willing to be put to death for telling others about Jesus. They would not have had such a deep conviction, even unto death, about something that was just a made-up fairy tale. They knew what they witnessed.

So here we are, more than 2,000 years later, and those who read the words of Jesus today also KNOW He is speaking truth. Even those who deny Jesus as God's Son acknowledge Jesus was wise and truthful. So, if Jesus was truthful in all other things, we can assume He was also truthful when saying He is God's Son and the Messiah.

WHAT DO YOU THINK?

➢ List all of the people Jesus appeared to after being raised from the dead, and count up how many people saw Jesus after he came back to life:

_____

_____

_____

_____

_____

_____

➢ How do you think the number of people who saw Jesus after His resurrection impacted the spread of Jesus's Good News about salvation and resurrection?

_____

_____

_____

_____

_____

➢ If we will all be judged by Jesus, what do you think will happen to all of those who go against Jesus and His teachings?

_____

_____

_____

_____

_____

_____

➢ From the first paragraph of this chapter, what do you need to hold to firmly for the sake of your salvation?

_____

_____

_____

_____

_____

➢ What does this chapter say will happen when the end time comes?

_____

_____

_____

_____

_____

➢ What do you want to happen to you when the end comes?

_____

_____

_____

_____

➢ Do you have any companions that corrupt your morals? If so, what do you think you should do in or about those relationships?

_____

_____

_____

_____

_____

_____

➤ According to this chapter, when the last trumpet sounds, what happens to death? And what will happen to Believers in Christ?

_____

_____

_____

_____

_____

➤ According to the last sentence in the chapter, what are we asked to do as we live and wait for God?

_____

_____

_____

_____

_____

➤ How can you live righteously, and what can you do to bear the image of Jesus Christ in your life?

_____

_____

_____

_____

_____

WHAT'S NEXT?

In the final chapter, which is next, I'll share some choices for the next steps you might want to take. You can decide what you'd like to know or do next. I'll share resources to help you get to know Jesus better and provide you with information about being saved by Jesus—if you aren't already.

WHAT'S NEXT?

Congratulations for completing the reading of the Gospel Book of Mark. Now that you've been introduced to Jesus, you might wonder, "What's next?"

If you've prayed a prayer turning your life over to Jesus, and asked him to come into your life as your lord and savior, then the next step is really getting to know Him. Everything Jesus taught us is important for your spiritual growth.

It's critical for you to study and get to know Jesus well. Too many people rely on what others tell them, and they don't ever get to know Jesus personally. Remember the passages about deceivers in the world? If you don't get to know Jesus personally, then you will be open to being deceived. Plus, Jesus can't be nearly as effective in your life if you don't develop a relationship with Him.

In Matthew 11:29-30, Jesus says, "*Take my yoke upon you, and learn from me, for I am gentle and lowly in heart, and you will find rest for your souls. For my yoke is easy, and my burden is light.*"

James 1:22-25 says, "Be doers of the Word, and not hearers only, deceiving yourselves. For if anyone is a hearer of the Word and not a doer, he is like a man who looks intently at his natural face in a mirror. For he looks at himself and goes away and at once forgets what he was like. But the one who looks into the perfect law, the law of liberty, and perseveres, being no hearer who forgets but a doer who acts, he will be blessed in his doing."

Studying Jesus will help build your faith in Him. Do you remember the teachings Jesus gave about how your faith affects the outcome of your prayers?

If you remember, you know it's important for you to have faith in Jesus in order to have effective prayers.

You can get to know Jesus well by reading each of the four main Gospel books in the New Testament. They are the Books of Matthew, Mark, Luke, and John. Each one will give you different insights into who Jesus is and what He taught.

The four Gospels cover Jesus' actions and teachings in detail. Mark and Luke give accounts of Jesus' life through the eyes of Jesus' disciples. Mark was the secretary who wrote Apostle Peter's eye-witness account; Luke, as a traveling companion of the Apostle Paul, thoroughly investigated Jesus. Matthew and John give their first-hand, eyewitness testimonies as Jesus' chosen disciples.

So what is your next step? How will you get to know Jesus better? What do you think are Jesus' expectations are, and what are your expectations for yourself?

My recommendation is to dive into a study of the Gospel of Matthew, titled: *Is Jesus the Savior?* As your next step. The study focuses on the prophecies in the Old Testament as they relate to Jesus.

Is Jesus the Savior? examines the prophecies which point toward Jesus, so you can decide for yourself whether you think the prophecies actually point to Jesus as the one and only Savior and true Son of God.

The Book of Matthew in the New Testament also explains Jesus's teachings in detail. A lot of Matthew's content comes directly from Jesus' teachings.

If you'd like a different study, you can check out the Journal Bible Studies listed on my website at JournalBibleStudy.com.

You can buy another Journal workbook to keep growing your knowledge. You can pick any study of the New or Old Testament, or just read your Bible directly.

Studying Jesus's teachings and God's expectations regularly is the best way to grow in unexpected ways and to get to know Jesus for who He really is.

May God bless you throughout your journey! May the Lord develop you into a strong, spirited child of God and follower of Jesus Christ!

DO YOU WANT TO BE SAVED BY JESUS?

If you haven't already asked Jesus to come into your life as your Savior, it's really easy to do. All you have to do is ask Jesus to be your Lord and Savior. Here's what the Bible says about being saved:

- **Romans 10:9-10** says, "If you will confess with your mouth that Jesus is Lord, and believe in your heart that God raised him from the dead, you will be saved. For with the heart, one believes unto righteousness; and with the mouth confession is made unto salvation."

- **Romans 10:13** says, "Whoever will call on the name of the Lord will be saved." The name of the Lord is Jesus.

- **Mark 16:16** says, "*He who believes and is baptized will be saved; but he who disbelieves will be condemned.*" Here, belief is the main key to being saved, but baptism is an act of faith for those who believe.

To be saved and have Jesus come into your life, it's as easy as believing Jesus is God's Son. With all sincerity, ask Jesus to save you and to become Lord in your life. You can do this easily by praying the following prayer:

> *"Lord Jesus, I believe you are God's Son, and God resurrected you from the dead. Please come into my life as my Lord and Savior, and save me from my sins. In Jesus' name I pray, Amen."*

For a deeper understanding of the concept of being saved, the book of John, Chapter 3:14-21 (quoted below) should help you. Keep in mind, when these verses refer to 'light,' they mean Jesus, because He is the Light to the world:

"As Moses lifted up the serpent in the wilderness, even so must the Son of Man (Jesus) be lifted up, that whoever believes in Him should not perish, but have eternal life. *For God so loved the world, that He gave His one and only Son (Jesus), that whoever believes in Him should not perish, but have eternal life.* For God didn't send His Son into the world to judge the world, but that the world should be saved through Him (Jesus). The person who believes in Him (Jesus) is not judged. The person who doesn't believe has been judged already, because he has not believed in the name of the one and only Son of God. This is the judgment, that the light (Jesus) has come into the world, and men loved the darkness rather than the light; for their works were evil. For everyone who does evil hates the light, and doesn't come to the light (Jesus), lest his works would be exposed. But he who does the truth comes to the light (Jesus), that his works may be revealed, that they have been done in God."

May God bless you in the days ahead as you seek Jesus, His truth, and light.

Going forward, I pray you will be greatly blessed whenever you spend time reading your Bible, praying, and fellowshipping with other believers. I pray you will find a church family you love, and you will seek to be baptized, if you haven't been already.

And remember always, if you prayed the prayer asking Jesus to be your Lord because you believe in Him, **you are saved**!

♥ CONGRATULATIONS! May God Bless YOU now and forever! ♥

ABOUT THE AUTHOR

Sandra K. Cook (a.k.a. Sandy) became a Christian when a door-to-door evangelism team came to tell her about Jesus. Sandy's life changed dramatically throughout the years that followed, although those changes didn't happen overnight.

Sandy was married at 19, widowed at the age of 22, lived in poverty, was assaulted, and a victim in a bank robbery, where she had a gun held to her head. In her early adulthood, Sandy was suicidal, struggled mightily with her self-esteem, and felt her life was pointless.

At the time of her first husband's death, Sandy began to read her Bible from cover-to-cover, deeply desiring to understand the purpose of life and to learn about God. Reading the Bible set Sandy's heart on walking with the Lord. She was gripped by the love God proclaims for each one of us, because she often felt unloved and unlovable.

In her life today, Sandy focuses on godly love, above all things, and seeks to help others feel and understand God's love, and to grow their fruit of the spirit. She believes everybody is more than just somebody... Everybody is God's Beloved Child, including YOU, my dear one!

The greatest joys in Sandy's life are spending time with her husband, sons, family, and her friends. Sandy loves reading to learn, studying the Bible, photography, and singing praise songs (although, you do not want to hear her tone deaf singing!)

Sandy earned her Degree of Divinity from the Christian Leaders Institute. She is a certified Biblical Life Coach, has a Master's Degree in Instructional Design, and is a life-long learner.

Sandy prays God will richly bless YOU in your life each and every day! ♥

OTHER BOOKS BY SANDY K. COOK

IS JESUS REAL?

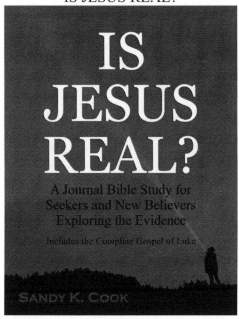

IS JESUS THE SAVIOR?

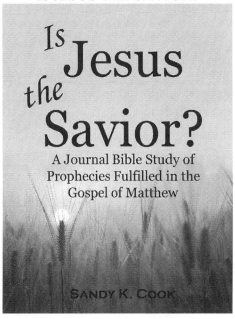

IS JESUS GOD?

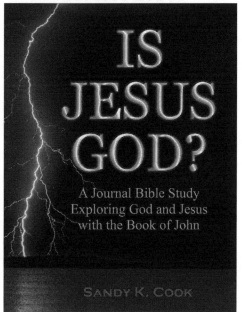

BE A PERSON AFTER GOD'S OWN HEART

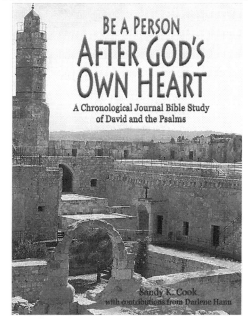

Made in United States
Troutdale, OR
10/26/2023